**ANDO**
ARCHITECT

Happy Birthday
Tarro !

from Anita +
Jason.

June 2001

# ANDO
## ARCHITECT

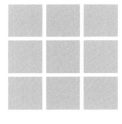

## KAZUKIYO MATSUBA

**PHOTOGRAPHY BY**
## TOMIO OHASHI

Translation
Lynne E. Riggs

Editorial Assistance
David B. Stewart

KODANSHA INTERNATIONAL
Tokyo • New York • London

Naoshima Contemporary Art Museum, Naoshima (above and frontispiece): submerged water court of the hotel wing

Distributed in the United States by Kodansha America, Inc., 114 Fifth Avenue, New York N.Y. 10011, and in the United Kingdom and continental Europe by Kodansha Europe Ltd., 95 Aldwych, London WC2B 4JF. Published by Kodansha International Ltd., 17-14 Otowa 1-chome, Bunkyo-ku, Tokyo 112-8652, and Kodansha America, Inc.

First edition, 1998
98 99 00 10 9 8 7 6 5 4 3 2 1
ISBN 4-7700-2171-2

# CONTENTS

# Ando in Current Perspective: Twenty Works 93

# POUNDING THE SANDBAG

Tadao Ando was born in Osaka, Japan, a major center of commerce and industry since ancient times. Growing up in a community of small manufacturers and industrial workshops, he internalized an ethic of hard work, family discipline, effort, and responsiblity. Given relative freedom as a small child, he matured into a strong individualist. His grandparents, with whom he lived and who brought him up, were both working people and did not goad him to achieve high marks at school. In the latter part of his school career Ando began training as an amateur boxer and by his senior year in high school became a certified professional. But after graduation he took up work as a draftsman in an architectural office. Unlike most architects whether in Japan or abroad, he did not go to university, but spent the 1960s—his twenties—learning to draft and traveling throughout Japan and abroad.

If Ando, a rugged individualist, appears not to conform to the stereotyped image of the Japanese, it is no wonder. He is an Osakaite, and Osakaites—indeed the inhabitants of the entire Kansai area in western Japan of which Osaka is the center—take pride in setting a standard of their own. Known for their business acumen and pragmatism, they are more uninhibited, whether in anger or joy, than the rather dry and generally reserved Tokyoites. Though possessing great self-discipline, they are not of the type to meekly follow authority. Disdaining "standard Japanese" as defined in the last century by the central government and today taught nationwide, they refuse to give up their own vernacular speech.

Ando is a person whose actions consistently conform to principle. He assumes full responsibility for the consequences of all he does and personally follows through on every detail. As has been famously noted in the national architecture press, he possesses an artisan's sophisticated sense of beauty—but also a self-identity committed to the modernist aesthetic—qualities that put him in a class by himself in Japan.

Although it might be an exaggeration to say that Japan is Tokyo, certainly some seventy percent of the national product is concentrated there, and the situation is similar in the field of construction. While not every ambitious American may think he or she has to aim for New York or Washington, Japanese do not ordinarily consider themselves to have arrived until they are established in Tokyo, no matter where they start out. Here again, Ando sticks to his guns; he has kept his main offices in Osaka since the beginning, launching from there a career that is now international.

Like his fellow Kansai-ites, Ando inevitably speaks with a distinctive Kansai intonation and manner, despite what anyone in Tokyo may happen to think of the "merchant city" of Osaka. Since late medieval times in Japan, the warrior and bureaucrat reaped honor and prestige, while the merchant was disdained, no matter how wealthy. Ando pays little attention to such niceties, and he has earned thereby a staunch following.

During the 1980s, as architectural fashion turned from rationalism and functionalism toward historical concerns in the guise of postmodernism, architects then seeking to establish themselves professionally faced a choice of sorts. There were, of course, those who criticized modernism in politically correct fashion, but the majority simply turned tail and followed the postmodernist crowd. In no time at all cityscapes around the world began to resemble a Disney skyline. But Ando was not among such perpetrators of kitsch; he remained dogged in his pursuit of modernism.

On more than one occasion European and American city planners and architects, or even artists, have praised Ando's devotion to modernism in my presence, not knowing that I am a close acquaintance. Many had ended up succumbing, albeit reluctantly, to the postmodernism tide; after all, society seemed to demand and decree it. They included architects and artists with reputations already established in the 1970s. They were, then, firm and genuine believers in modernism who gave up their ideals, but they are proud of Ando, who does not bow to passing trends. Undiverted from his path, he is a person they trust to carry on the mission they felt forced to abandon.

From the earliest concrete box (the less than 1,000-square-foot Row House Sumiyoshi) that launched his career, Ando has continued to stake everything on abstract geometry and beauty of proportions. He then rallies as many people as possible to his cause by explaining his architecture in every way he can. Ultimately, however, what guarantees the success of each building is his mastery of geometry that sustains a superb sense of proportion—which only Ando is able to achieve.

In short, Ando carries on his pursuit of modernist beauty, regardless of how the world of architecture around him may change, or the fickleness of others. It goes nearly without saying that modernism is a form of idealism, while postmodernism simply caters to a world of whims. In the realm of communication, Ando is considerate: unlike many architects, he listens to the needs of his clients, and responds softly in his distinctive Kansai drawl. But in daily work, he is the "creator" and is unlikely to bend his principles. It is this committed stance that has won the acclaim of creative professionals around the world.

It has been my observation that those architects who attain greatness have undergone three formative transformations in the course of their lives. This was true of Kenzo Tange, who started from an aesthetic of traditional *sukiya* architecture (his own house reflects the style of Katsura Imperial Villa), blossomed in dynamic metastructures, and later turned to elegant postmodern Déco. Mies van der Rohe was a possible exception, but the careers of Le Corbusier and I. M. Pei also illustrate the three-stage development. As for Ando, it is my belief that he is currently in the second phase.

Ando's works have not changed at core; there remains the reinforced-concrete box. But since around the time of the Raika Building, his focus has significantly shifted toward the environment and, above all, the surrounding landscape. His concrete apparitions rise up in exquisitely fine proportions before expanses of green landscape or open ocean, microcosmic observation towers from which to appreciate the features of land or sea.

One of the public's greatest grievances against contemporary architecture has been the insistence on isolation and on being original and novel to the bitter end. Ando has long been aware of the city's natural potential; witness his first work, Row House Sumiyoshi—which summoned its users into intimate contact with the weather. Still, the more perfect the solid concrete box, the stronger its impression of being deliberately introspective and closed to the outside. But now, more recent works appear to have razed this self-imposed barrier. Ando's latest work is consciously open to the environment, and to the landscape.

Perhaps people like myself, positioned to observe his recent works close at hand here in Japan, see Ando in a particular light, and somewhat larger in scale as a designer than overseas admirers who may be familiar mainly with earlier works. But already his second phase is on the verge of developing into a third one. Ando, in a work to be located abroad and now under design, is in the process of revealing a third ethos.

When I heard that Tadao Ando had won the competition for the new Modern Art Museum of Ft. Worth, Texas, I was extremely pleased. It meant his work was now recognized as having potential far beyond the building of the scrupulously crafted classical concrete box. The series of oblong exhibition halls reflecting the roofline of the adjacent Kimbell Museum of Art by Louis I. Kahn seems the product of Ando's reading of the environmental context. In this new work, moreover, he surrounds his concrete with a glass skin, thereby positing the beauty of a new material. All in all we see the approach of a third phase.

As I write, news has arrived that Ando has been named to the Faculty of Architecture of the University of Tokyo. This university is the pinnacle of Japan's academy, and has produced many of the best known Japanese architects, Kenzo Tange and Arata Isozaki to cite only two. But Tadao Ando has no formal training in architecture; in fact he is viewed in Japan as a kind of anti-hero vis-à-vis the academy. That such a man should be appointed professor at the country's top-ranking national university, given the stuffy, myopic character of the Japanese establishment, is no less than a revolution.

In fact, the field of architecture is not one that really suits the educational philosophy of this former imperial university known for turning out a high-achieving academic elite, many of whom proceed to lifetime careers in the national bureaucracy. Nevertheless, it is readily believed that the cream of young people hoping to pursue careers in architecture end up at this institution. Now, Ando is to become one of its professors.

I might also add that only an acute sense of crisis could have inspired the University of Tokyo to seat a maverick like Ando on its faculty. As is sometimes the case elsewhere, Japan's universities are filled with teaching staff who cannot adapt to contemporary realities. Japanese as a whole are suffering from a still-dim awareness that our country may have undertaken more economic responsibility than we are capable of sustaining. This realization has even begun to affect education, and a severe sense of future anxiety hangs over Japanese society like a dark cloud. No doubt Ando's appointment reflects the desperate search for talent capable of vanquishing that cloud.

Winning the Modern Art Museum of Ft. Worth competition and promotion to the faculty of the University of Tokyo have made 1997 a turning point for Tadao Ando. These events place Osaka's hometown hero firmly on the path toward becoming a world-renowned architect, and a representative of Japan in the truest sense.

An aura of myth surrounds Ando's career. The tale of how he obtained a professional boxing license in his high school years—and even entered the ring in Thailand—has played a significant role in mythologizing the man's image. One cannot help being reminded of the story of the boy who grew up by the strength of his fighting arm in the streets of Brooklyn and went on to become world champion. But there is certainly something irresistable about this Osaka champion who has gone on pummeling the sandbag, so to speak, throughout his architectural career. He has pounded tirelessly at the closed nature of Japanese society, which oppresses even those inside it, as if to emphasize how few Japanese individuals of real character there are in leading positions in the world today. Once the sound of Ando's gloves pounding the sandbag echoes beyond the back rowhouses of Osaka and resounds around the world, I believe that Japan's true artistic integrity will measure up to anyone's, anywhere in the world.

# Twenty-Year
# Acquaintance
# Revisited

# AFFINITY FOR CRAFTSMANSHIP
## To Treviso, Italy

▦

Asummer breeze now swept through the window of the Mercedes that Kuriki was driving through the north Italian countryside. The weather was hot. The previous night, at a café in front of the Fenice Theater in Venice, the stone pavement had still radiated the day's heat, wilting my usually vigorous appetite as I waited to be served.

Earlier I had taken a water taxi from the wharf in front of my hotel on the Grand Canal as far as the station plaza, where Kuriki picked me up. Masashi Kuriki was a witty and entertaining conversationalist. He had been a trading-company manager stationed in Italy when he quit to take charge of public relations for the apparel-maker Benetton's Milan office. The Mercedes was equipped with a hands-free telephone, and as we drove along Kuriki consulted his staff in a rhythmic melody of Italian that was pleasing even to my uncomprehending ear.

Venice behind us, we headed for Treviso. This is the homeland of the Benetton empire, where its company headquarters and most of its factories are located. We were going to Treviso to visit Fabrica, the new art school being built there under Tadao Ando's direction.

As we sped along the expressway, the telephone rang.

"Would you like to talk to him?" Kuriki asked me. "It's from Chicago."

"All right," I said, picking up the receiver.

"Yano here. I'm with Ando in Chicago. Is everything all right?" said the voice at the other end.

"Absolutely. Mr. Kuriki has taken care of things splendidly," I answered. Masataka Yano has managed Ando's projects on site since long before his boss became so well known. He had at various times shown me around more than ten of Ando's works. I had planned this trip to see Fabrica on rather short notice and asked Yano to make the arrangements. Aware that we would be on our way to Treviso at that particular hour, he had called to verify how things had worked out.

The relationship between an architect and a critic like myself can be a delicate one. An architect, needless to say, is a master creator of enduring edifices. A critic who makes his living from journalistic scribblings cannot help but feel a bit jealous of someone capable of putting up structures that change the complexion of the landscape. A distinguished architect is thus a creature who fills the critic with both awe and envy.

Of course, the critic has something going for him as well. Architecture, rooted in the soil, is by definition an immobile art. It would be unknown without the critic, whose writings can be transmitted to the ends of the earth.

Tadao Ando and I have thus jostled against each other a fair amount as we pursued our respective professions over the past twenty years. Sometimes we do not agree. There are a few buildings by Ando I have deliberately not written about. But I always come back when he produces his next one, drawn by an irresistible pull that erases any temporary estrangement.

For some reason, as I sped through the Italian countryside during that inordinately hot summer of 1995 chatting with Yano in Chicago, my mind kept going back to the Kansai area, where both Ando and I were born and raised: I recalled downtown Osaka and moments from visits to Ando's works in the tidy suburbia between Osaka and Kobe.

We had both come a long way from those days when we sauntered around the streets of Kobe, trading jibes and discussing Ando's newest work. I was here in Italy, and Ando's latest projects were now being built in Chicago and Treviso. What impressed me was not so much the way Ando handles work in different parts of the world. Since the beginning of the 1990s, working overseas has ceased to be a novelty for Japanese architects. Rather my chat with Yano reminded me how important to such projects are the trusted, experienced staff of the architect.

I returned the receiver to Kuriki. As another call came in from somewhere else, he began to talk in Italian again. Being from an area of Japan where the dialect is typically rapid and dense, I found the rollicking rhythm and sheer quantity of talk extremely pleasing, a soothing assurance that this pilgrimage to see Ando's work would be enjoyable.

With such expectations, I started to relax. Affected by the fatigue of my journey, I grew drowsy.

The town of Treviso where we were headed may not mean much to most non-Italians. The nearest well-known city is Venice. Before I was even sure how to reach Treviso, I had left Japan and taken a hotel in Venice. According to Kuriki's explanation, Treviso was once a summer resort where Venetian aristocrats went to escape the heat.

In contrast to Venice, the "city of canals," Treviso is covered entirely with cobblestones and pavement, a provincial capital surrounded by pastoral hills. In former days this was a silk-producing region, Kuriki said, which explains the large sheds once used for raising silkworms. We left the expressway and moved along country roads, fields stretching out on either hand. We sped onward through a lazy, relatively undistinguished rural landscape.

Fabrica, the art school being built under the patronage of Luciano Benetton, is intended to bring together young people with some previous art training and encourage them in creative work for the future.

Students are not subject to short-term deadlines or material results. Instead, the idea behind the school is an expectation that activities there may contribute to the kind of firm Benetton ought to be in the twenty-first century. It is thus an investment. If marketable ideas arise, they will be incorporated into new products, but the spirit of Fabrica is, above all, to transcend the mundane. The school is seen as offering a design challenge for the future.

## No Ordinary Client

Japanese have a fairly clear image of Luciano Benetton, who in one generation has built his company into a global concern. One can tell at a glance from Benetton's aggressive and artistic image-fostering posters that its founder is no ordinary businessman. He caught the whole world off balance when he posed in the nude for one of them. Then again, his deliberately diverse choice of models reflecting our multicultural age has had a strong impact in times like these when Europe's cities are torn by inter-ethnic violence. We can only respect the keenly contemporary conscience of such a firm. It was this man who picked Ando for his special project. It is not unusual, all the same, for the founder-owners of successful businesses to seek out the services of an avant-garde architect.

In order to bring a building to completion, all manner of requirements have to be met before it takes final shape. In the case of Ando, a private architect, it was first necessary to persuade the client, that is, Benetton, to accept his artistic ideas and concepts. Next, the contractor is chosen and countless on-site problems have to be dealt with and solved. Only then can the "box"—or shell—of a building emerge.

The client sets many demands on the practical use of this box, and the architect exercises a partial power of yea or nay as he pursues the kind of space he believes ideal. If the architect is finally able to strike a delicate balance between fulfilling the client's functional demands and exciting the user's imagination, he has created a masterpiece. It is in this realm between function and imagination that the architect struggles with the tasks of design development and construction supervision—while aiming for the ideal.

The intensity of the struggle is the greater in proportion to the architect's commitment to his profession. But no matter how conscientiously he strives, a building is inevitably the target of discussion and debate; it is subjected to a sort of public trial. In the face of such criticism, the only person in a position to withstand the fusillade is the client who has commissioned the work. The only way to salvage the reputation of a building projected on the basis of ideas ahead of its time is for the patron to ignore criticism, making it clear that since he or she is paying, no one else is entitled to find fault.

Clients who engage the services of avant-garde architects are very often of a dubious sort, like scions of the American nouveau riche or real estate developers who fueled the the recent Japanese "bubble" economy. What category does Luciano Benetton fall into? Judging from his posters, he is clearly a man who would take little interest in a building enterprise so ordinary that it attacted neither praise nor censure.

Benetton is constantly issuing challenges. He is noted for his casual line of mass-market fashions aimed specifically at young people. The posters consciously provoke, as if designed to keep the company young and vital. In that sense, Benetton was a client amply qualified to choose Tadao Ando.

Why did Benetton select Ando? By his own account, he believes Ando is the appropriate figure to forge a union between history and the future. It hardly needs saying that Italy is the heartland of architecture and the arts. Even at the proud and prestigious École des Beaux-Arts in Paris, the most coveted honor remains the "Rome Prize," a scholarship to study in Italy. Indeed, it would not be an overstatement to call Paris a

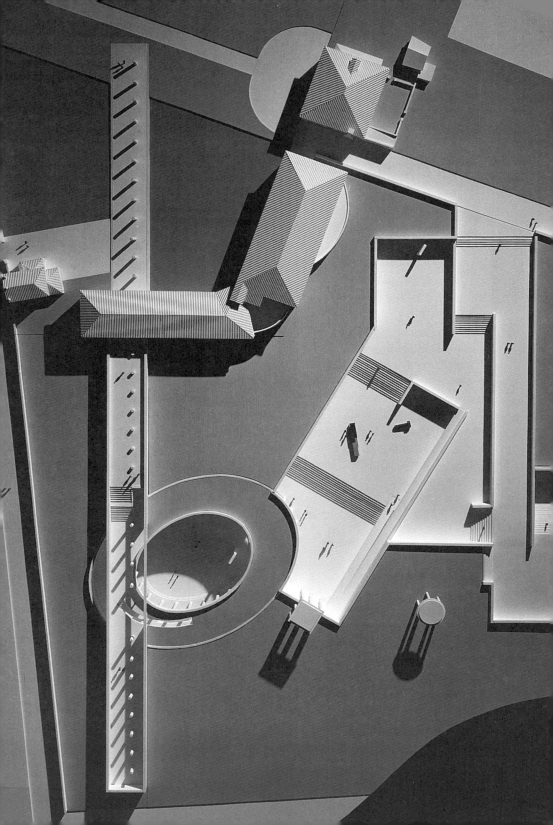

replica of Rome. Naturally, the impact of Italy's cultural glories is felt not only beyond its borders but within the country as well.

I remember how the well-known industrial designer Mario Bellini emphasized the tremendous respect accorded to architects in Italy and insisted that he was not merely a designer but first of all an architect. He had even learned the Japanese word for architect, *kenchikuka*, and repeated it over and over when introducing himself in Japan.

I admit I was slightly disconcerted to find an artist of Bellini's caliber so obsessed with the status of architect. No doubt this has to do with the fact that in order to change even a tiny part of an Italian city, one must inevitably do battle with history. That makes the demands imposed on an architect substantially different in Japan and Italy. It was in the natural course of things that Benetton should ask Ando to preserve the history accumulated at Treviso, and the task, imposed by a unique client, weighed heavily on Ando's shoulders.

From Bellini's standpoint, it might be enviable to be an architect of established world renown like Ando. But there in the Italian countryside, Ando was suddenly immersed in an ambiguous struggle as a contemporary designer. Now I was going to see what that struggle had produced.

## Villa of Dreams

Here in northern Italy, the rural landscape is much like that to be seen throughout Europe; it stretches beneath slightly clouded blue skies from horizon to horizon. In the countryside about an hour's drive north of Venice, on the outskirts of the graceful provincial city of Treviso where the rich once built their summer villas, we find attractive, comfortable-looking farms. It is hard to believe that the aggressive, restless Benetton should have made his home base in this quiet, relaxed rural setting.

The teaming up of Benetton and Ando since 1992 is nothing if not provocative. Fabrica will serve as the dauntless Benetton's flagship for charting new frontiers in art and fashion. European devotees of Ando's work eager to see his architecture firsthand have been curious to know what he will produce for such a client.

Drawing near the Benetton estate, outside Treviso, we came upon a group of young people. Dressed with the casual stylishness of aspiring artists, they were clearly not local. We greeted them, and upon hearing

◀ Fabrica, Treviso: site model with colonnade at left

Fabrica: restoration (seventeenth century) and reflecting pool

where we were headed, they smiled. So these were the students of Fabrica, the talent expected to carry the Benetton enterprise into the future.

Fabrica is a villa of dreams where the present encounters history, embodied in the old villa left standing on the site. The *present* is the architecture wrought by Tadao Ando. The challenge Ando accepted was to incorporate a historical edifice into an architectural complex serving as a milestone toward the future.

We approached the vast site from the rear, directly behind the old villa itself. Shadows cut across the blazing summer sunshine. In one corner, we could see a carpenter working quietly alone, stripped to the waist. Unconcerned with whoever might be approaching, he seemed to be adjusting wooden forms for concrete. Watching such workmen at their labors is, for me, a favorite sight in Europe.

Unlike big-scale construction projects in the United States and Japan, milling with scores of laborers, in Europe one is more likely to see only small numbers at work, steadily but usually not in great haste. Entrusting themselves to the easy flow of time, they work carefully and methodically. Nor, day by day, do they alter their pace, even to produce a contemporary building. They take on Ando's reinforced-concrete scheme and set it in place for the next thousand years. And, indeed, there are few more gratifying experiences than the sight of form thus being created for eternity by human hands. Surely that is what Ando had asked for on this project. Watching this man's hands at work made me feel that success was already assured.

Indeed, the success of Ando's architecture has almost invariably been an extension of skilled craftsmanship. But since the craftsmen in most cases had been Japanese, I was concerned about what might happen when he attempted to build outside Japan. Ando had triumphed in the Japan Pavilion for the World Expo at Seville, an innovative wooden construction. The poured concrete that is the essence of Ando's architecture requires still more substantial skill. The distinctive European aura of earnest worksmanship embodied in that lone carpenter bending to his labors inside the Fabrica grounds banished my worries and instilled a sense of confidence. Here, we could be certain, was craft as fine as any to be found in Japan.

The scene we encountered as we rounded the side of the old mansion and emerged in front was dazzling. Beneath the merciless sun, a portrait of water, light, and open space—past and present—spread with splendid integrity before us. The core of the old aristocratic villa is a two-story timber frame edifice with neoclassical detail in what is called the Palladian style. Palladio was, of course, the sixteenth-century mason's son who pioneered new ideas in building design inspired by Roman architecture, bringing about a virtual revolution both in northern Italy and the world. I admit to being skeptical of the extent to which such a villa remains faithful to Palladio's inspiration and style, but the very mention of the great architect's name is, above all, testimony to the tremendous pride Treviso takes in its traditions. At Fabrica, Ando had to confront the challenge of this deep-seated local pride.

The walls of the villa were cream-colored stucco, whose soft tones shimmered coolly on the surface of the new reflecting basin built to Ando's design. Since leaving the commotion of Venice, I had seen nothing so soothing to the spirit as its quiet surface. The effect was magnificent. The villa itself, a relic of the latter seventeenth century though it may be, is hardly more than a rather undistinguished country house. It was only with the addition of this sheet of water that it acquired elegance.

The reflected silhouette of the villa is all the more refreshing in the rustic sunlight. Recalling the fervor Roman emperors invested to replicate the universe in their palace gardens, it is at the same time reminiscent of the refinements of houses and gardens in Japan halfway round

Fabrica: colonnade viewed from existing arcade

Fabrica: colonnade surrounded by water

the world. Ando's success with the integration of water and architectural form showed itself first in 1990 in the Garden of Fine Arts he designed for the Osaka Flower Expo. The dialogue between landscape and building created by water amid the wasteland-like exposition site had at last found its true home here in the somnambulent landscape of northern Italy. I marveled at the resourcefulness of the architect here in a foreign land.

A row of columns marches diagonally across the pool on a slab set just above water level—like the *hashigakari* passage leading to a Noh stage—boldly slicing through the symmetry created by the villa and pool. Against the gentle, traditional landscape, the juxtaposition of harmony and its interruption strikes a pleasing tension. The height of these columns is aligned with the villa's second story, carefully calculated to echo the scale of the villa as reflected in the water.

## History and Contemporaneity Enhanced

The bare concrete pillars Ando erected effect a cold, stark twentieth-century modernism, completely different from the warm, creamy handcrafted texture of the neoclassical villa. One would have thought the two would be dissonant. The columned causeway cutting through the pool ought to have clashed with the original architecture, yet the scene before me was the embodiment of harmony. Was it simplistic to attribute such harmony to the scale of the pillars? That couldn't be all. I could sense the manifest respect paid to history, but not in a shape that simply froze and preserved it. Ando had indeed captured the grandeur of tradition in the height of his columns, attaining a harmony of past and present in the line of columns moving across the water. The ensemble was a condensed statement of the contemporary architect's reverence for history.

The effort to preserve and restore, while resurrecting the whole as a contemporary functional building, is also being attempted at the main corporate headquarters located a short distance away. While respect for history is weightiest at the headquarters, Ando shows at Fabrica that he stands his ground in the contemporary, albeit there, too, the modern has been subtly modulated alongside the historical.

I saw what that meant as I explored the interior of the villa. The pale pink stucco of its halls is stunning, especially when one is accus-

Fabrica: seventeenth-century trusses in studio

tomed mostly to the bare concrete walls for which the architect is best known. That luscious finish is even to be found on the walls of the egg-shaped atrium, the most dramatic space within the complex. The elliptical aperture let into the floor is strongly reminiscent of the ovoid volume first conceived for the second Nakanoshima project, Osaka, and later echoed in the design of Inamori Hall, Kagoshima University. Much to the surprise of everyone familiar with Ando's work, he adopted stucco walls firmly tied to local Italian tradition.

Here it may be that the geometry would have emerged more sharply had the finish been plainer. But the architect did not choose this, and the decision must have been made in deference to history. Or, perhaps, I thought to myself, Ando chose to finish the walls in traditional style out of appreciation for the artisans I had just seen at work behind the main building.

Ando is an architect attentive to the sites where his projects are unfolding and to the workmen laboring there. Observing the preservation and restoration of older architecture in Venice, you notice at once the great pride Italian artisans take in their traditional crafts. This profound respect for history must have struck a responsive chord with Ando. No doubt he reflected that the stucco technique and other local skills passed down by these craftsmen were too pleasing a gift of history to ignore.

There are many signs within of the precedence given to history. In the atelier arranged on the top floor of the building beneath its exposed roof beams, the ingenuity of traditional joinery is visible in all its robust glory. Here space is unadorned; plain, unpainted wood invites an asceticism well-suited to training and study. I observed young people at computers exploring the Internet while others sketched, each pursuing an individual path of creativity.

In contrast to the historicism that pervaded architecture in the 1980s—reducing all kinds of structures to superficial trappings of amusement-park indolence—the interior at Benetton is practical and serviceable, as befits a place for study and creativity. The traces of Ando's hand are almost imperceptible here, the assertion of his personal taste withheld in favor of respect for the dignity of the materials that bore the original structure over the centuries. His choice is unerring. Then, once more in the corridors outside the atelier—and throughout the building, even to its toilets—the beauty of restored stucco reigns supreme. The stark contrast, I realized admiringly, works to enhance the tension and concentration in the atelier space.

There had been a change of mayors in Treviso, causing delay in construction. The underground section of the project, situated behind the old building, had yet to be finished. The row of columns, rising out of the pool in the main courtyard, already marched straight through the interior of the first floor of the restored villa; once the construction beyond is complete, it will extend all the way to the above-grade portion of the sunken structure to be built there. The subterranean area of the design includes a library and gallery facing a toplit courtyard.

Ando has executed a number of plans for structures below grade, as he feels that underground spaces are ideal for realizing an architecture of pure proportions. Observing recent developments in his work, we can see how well the underground solution merges each structure harmoniously with the existing environment. Within an existing environment, an architect must impose a creation that embodies his strongest convictions—a source of internal turmoil for many architects. Even Ando, the author of many buildings for downtown metropolitan areas, is continually expected to discover ways to do this, no matter how chaotic or wanting in inspiration the surroundings. On the other hand, Ando's affinity for underground solutions also works well in spacious natural surroundings, as first seen in the Children's Museum, Hyogo—a testimony to his increased stature as a public architect.

Indeed, Ando's works since the 1990s can be described as *ground* architecture. He has significantly restrained his expression of the structure as *figure*, or volume, and stressed respect for the background against which a building is set, whether ocean or land. In this we observe Ando's critical stance with regard to the vast outpouring of "postmodernist" architecture that was far too inclined to focus on figure, wreaking havoc with environmental context. Ando's works, set within the natural landscape, deemphasize figure to the utmost, pursuing rather the configuration of the land itself by extending their architectural roots deep beneath the surface. We may also interpret such works as his critique of the frivolity and rootlessness of the present age.

Fabrica is part of this recent lineage of Ando works. In the expansive setting of the quiet north Italian countryside, he eschews obtrusive expression, devoting himself to the serene creation of his own universe in this gentle context, as if in conscious submission to the proverbial "when in Rome . . . ." Once the entire project is complete, people will no doubt visit the Palladian villa first—drawn to it by natural impulse. And then, proceeding further into the heart of the subterranean complex, they will come face to face with Ando's universe in its purest form.

Europe's appraisal of Ando is astronomical. His "Meditation Space" for the UNESCO headquarters building in Paris has drawn increasing attention. It is remarkable that an architect born and raised in the atmosphere of a place like Osaka should be accorded so much renown on the other side of the globe. Ando himself remains modest. The greater his pride of native place, the deeper his respect for other lands, and the stronger his committed attention to the murmurings of the earth.

It may be bizarre to suggest a similarity between Osaka, that time-honored center of Japanese commerce and industry, and Italy, where it is said that every household is also a factory. And yet I felt in the northern Italian countryside, once a hub of the silk industry, a heritage long forgotten in Osaka. My intuition that Fabrica would be a success came from my conviction that a common feeling had helped Ando to relax and create in this place, so far removed from his familiar element, a work of impressive scale and freewheeling imagination.

# AN ENTHUSIASM FOR CREATION
## To Himeji

███
███
███

Ⓞne holiday in early autumn, in the
wake of heavy typhoon rains, we met near the railway station at Himeji. We were going to tour Ando's recent Children's Museum (1989)
located in Hyogo prefecture. Before I set foot in the hotel restaurant at
the appointed time, I heard Ando's hearty welcome. Those gentle, irresistible Kansai tones are his leading punch—unchanged in the twenty
years I have known him. Early in our relationship we discovered, in a
casual conversation, that we had both lived in the same neighborhood
of Nishinomiya, between Osaka and Kobe, at around the same time.
The Kansai dialect has a quality that softens the edges of any abrasive
comment and disarms a listener's defenses against the speaker, and I
am especially susceptible to its charms. Ando may now be firmly ensconced in the company of world-class architects, but he has never lost
the friendly manner that makes people immediately open up to him,
even at a first meeting.

In the Himeji area, we visited two works by Ando. One was the
Children's Museum and the other the Himeji Museum of Literature
(1991), still under construction. Both are splendid examples of how creativity can soar, wings full spread, in dialogue with the land. But what
for me was particularly pleasant about these visits was witnessing the
friendship and warmth with which everyone we encountered greeted
Ando.

We had arrived at the museum unannounced and intended to depart
just as unobtrusively. But as we were on our way out of the museum
grounds, the director came running down the long slope Ando de-

Children's Museum, Hyogo: detail of main facility overlooking the lake

signed as an approach; she was out of breath, but apparently had no particular business to discuss. She simply wanted to express her gratitude for his visit. She was all smiles and genuinely pleased that Ando had come.

At the literature museum, the twenty-odd helmeted workers ceased their work to accompany Ando around the site. I have visited many construction projects with other architects, but have never experienced anything like this before or since. Most prominent architects tend to be remote figures prone to obscure philosophizing, rather beyond the reach of the people laboring on their buildings. The workers behave distantly toward such architects, partly out of respect, but also because architects as a tribe are considered outsiders to the nitty-gritty affair of construction. However, the atmosphere of the site at Himeji was visibly enlivened by Ando's appearance. He greeted the construction supervisor and general contractor with a friendly Kansai-dialect salutation, *"Do nai ya?"* (How's it going?).

When Ando issues orders to his office staff, his tone is stentorian, but when he turns to speak to others, he is beaming and kind. The warm reception I observed at the museum site is the product of the trust Ando has earned among people working at his projects. They are eager for the chance to show Ando their handiwork, and they display pride at participating in one of his buildings. Responding to expectations, Ando strolls around the site, going over each point—his manner gentle, but serious and uncompromising—making sure things meet with his requirements.

"Look here," Ando calls out to me, standing in front of a slit-like window. "A good view of Himeji castle."

"That sure gave us a hard time, all thanks to you," interjects a worker from the side.

To which Ando glances back, grinning, "Well, maybe so. But isn't it fine!"

And so a jocular repartee entertains the twenty or so people on the project tagging along behind us. This relationship between architect and construction staff is something for which the citizens of this area, the real owners and users of this new public facility, can be grateful. When those working on the project are excited and proud, the client can be sure of a good job, one that reflects the original intent of the design. Because of this, people think of Ando as different from the brand of architect who spouts difficult abstractions and acts the lofty personage. I could see that this building, too, had inspired that happy relationship between architect and local citizen.

Children's Museum: detail of the promenade

## The Architect au Naturel

Tadao Ando today maintains an easy and relaxed attitude toward what he does. He did not yet have this admirable composure in the 1970s when he rocketed onto the architectural scene as an anti-establishment boxer-turned-architect, or in the 1980s as he gradually established his reputation. The hard-fighting spirit he had cultivated as a boxer stood him in good stead against the absurdities he encountered in professional life; with blood, sweat, and tears he finally attained the conviction needed to survive the unanchored age of the 1990s. It is this open-minded, relaxed stance that leads me to believe we can expect still more from him in the future.

While he is sometimes idolized on account of his success-story rise from obscurity, I can only congratulate Ando on casting off this label, one that would have permitted him to rest on his laurels. Certainly he must have wished for the aura of success, as anyone might. When you find your work suddenly an object of praise and center of attention, it is easy enough to lose sight of who you are.

Architecture is a long, drawn-out battle with a host of conventional practices. In the shadow of what appears a glamorous profession, architects struggle with despondency, anger, and fatigue. The celebrated "aura" is the tempter promising relief from the sense of isolation their labors engender. As the aura descends like a halo upon the architect, his rank advances, but should he allow its presence to intoxicate? Trapped within the spell of professional acclaim, the architect begins to issue incomprehensible declarations and indulge in self-aggrandizing talk. This tendency, I believe, is the source of a deep-rooted distaste for architects among the Japanese public.

And what about Ando? In the early 1980s, his office was still located in Osaka's downtown Honmachi district. Partly because there wasn't much space I often watched him deal directly with clients. At the time, though already considered an architect of promise, he was not yet all that well known. His clients were rarely public organizations, but mainly small businesses, such as confectioners, based in the Kansai area. In a friendly atmosphere, he would meet with them, going over even the finest points of the plans with care, chatting in the easygoing Kansai manner. I was fond of the atmosphere of Ando's Honmachi office. It feels now like a long time ago, and it is hard to remember the exact quality, but I clearly recall the restraint and modesty that reigned there.

Ando's Kansai speech does seem to be one of the tools that elevat-

Children's Museum: wading pool adjacent to main facility

ed him to godly status, but when I remember the rippling drawl that echoed through that Honmachi office, I am reminded anew that Ando is a natural. He is not a poser. Whatever others may think, Ando himself has never sought the architect's aura, and I think he quickly and instinctively perceived the danger of losing himself to its spell. In the Honmachi office days, Ando frequently made the rounds of projects being built in the city, and though he might go out with unexpected visitors like myself, he always returned to the office in the evening. "I have to set a good example for the young folk," he would tell me; "an office without the boss around will never amount to anything."

At that time, on the eve of the bubble economy, architects in Tokyo were busy in many ways. It is a curious phenomenon that almost all Japanese architects consider themselves ideologues of one sort or other. They like lecture engagements and aspire to be treated as men or women of culture by the media. They often write abstruse essays for publication in professional journals. Ando will lecture or write articles if asked, but from what I have observed, he is far more energetic and alive while walking around a construction site than on a podium or before a microphone. Hearing him talk about his work, I am always convinced that here is a person who really likes architecture.

Of the many architects of my acquaintance, I have a feeling there are very few with a genuine affinity for architecture. One thinks of Kenzo Tange, who will bring out photos and models and can talk endlessly about his works. Likewise, you have to believe in Arata Isozaki, who never fails to set architectural history in contemporary perspective. But they are the minority. What most architects like is something other than architecture. In fact, I am often amazed to notice that what these architects like best of all is the status of being an architect; they want nothing more than to be a sought-after expert on art and culture.

By contrast, Ando has continuously pressured himself to be a working architect. He used to say that the head of a design firm should never draw a salary more than twice that of the best paid office employee. Working conditions in a Japanese architectural firm, by the way, are not particularly good, and in an office like Ando's in the early 1980s, when the boss as well as the staff were all young, the wages of the staff could not have been more than ¥5 million (about $45,000) a year. If, as he advocated, Ando's salary at the time was no more than twice that, his earnings were modest, indeed, considering the work and time he put in. Of course, expenses for trips abroad and other company-related activities were covered. Still, from pronouncements like this, I believe that

◀ Children's Museum: glazed section of wall overlooking park

Ando pushed himself to sustain the hard-working, "hungry" spirit responsible for his success.

# Man of Principle

Ando is almost too strict in the standards he sets for his staff. He once told me he had made a young employee who had been treated to a cup of coffee by a contractor go back and pay for it. The firm in question could have been either a big general contractor or a small local building firm. In any case, the work of an architect is chiefly design and supervision. The design part may be fairly straightforward, but the supervision aspect of architectural work in Japan is intense—a fact not widely known or understood.

Roughly speaking, the architect produces a design in accordance with the client's brief and then selects a builder by putting the work out to bid. The contractor is obligated to carry out the construction in accordance with the architect's design blueprints. The architect, for his part, is required to make sure, on behalf of the client, that the builder is using materials, following construction methods, and attending to all details as specified. All this work comes under the title of supervision.

So, even though an architect's office may only have twenty or so staff, it has to be prepared to deal with the people from mammoth general contracting firms, for in principle the architects are in charge of the project. Ando believes the architectural side should have sufficient pride of position to refuse even a cup of coffee. He believes in the principle of this relationship. Of course, everyone in architecture knows the reality, for it is the big general contractors who in practice exercise the power and control. Still, for an employee to deviate in matters of principle is something Ando will never tolerate.

This is a philosophy one can admire. There are plenty of clients who must scrimp and save to bring their project to fruition. They come to an architect with the task of building a home—likely the greatest outlay of a lifetime. Their expectation is that the power of Ando's design will change their lives. But before this lofty ideal can be realized, all the inglorious tasks of supervision have to be performed. Architects may not stress this aspect of their work, but it is clear that without strict attention to detail a building cannot be completed. Ando believes this to be the first item his staff must be made aware of. His strict treatment of these young people is the product of his awareness of himself as leader.

At one point, I remember, Ando frequently alarmed me by advocating the tactics of "teaching by fear." Apparently he came up with this notion out of a conviction that it was good for people never to be allowed to let down their guard. There's the story of Ando's becoming upset with a new employee for wasting paper in the process of preparing construction documents, and he made her stand holding a pile of paper for several hours to teach her a lesson. Whether she stood there for the allotted time is uncertain, for apparently she burst out crying, but surely the punishment was too severe.

The story is often told, not out of criticism of Ando, but in admiration. Part of the broad support he enjoys comes from the fact that he will not give in to the tendency toward leniency and overindulgence rampant in Japan today. Although age once implied authority in Japan, this changed radically after World War II, and most older people have long since ceased to frown on, much less scold, inappropriate behavior on the part of the young. This fact has unmistakably eroded one good aspect of Japanese society. Nursing serious misgivings about the moral fiber of Japan from his corner of the city of Osaka, Ando decided that he would do what he could as a single individual to reverse the tide. This continues to be reflected in his strict treatment of staff.

While Ando may have acquired a reputation for settling such matters somewhat harshly, some people welcome this approach. When I visited the office building Sun Place, for example, I heard how he had used fisticuffs with one of the construction workers. By all accounts, the story was circulating as a kind of legend, told with pride, of the time Ando "did the guy in." This is a strange way to create a hero, but as I saw at the Himeji Museum of Literature, quite a few people take simple pleasure in being able to share time with Ando precisely because of who and what he is.

In the final analysis, people only trust those who are genuine. Society places confidence in what is real and honest. Besides, Ando achieves things no one else can, and he has thus amassed a social credibility that is earning him ever increasing numbers of personal supporters.

Watching Ando grow into an important presence in the architectural world, I have felt his success almost frightening, but his view of life seems to me to present a virtual guidepost for society. The trip to Himeji lent strength to my conviction.

Museum of Literature, Himeji: with view of Himeji Castle in distance

# TRANSMIGRATION OF FORMS

To Rokko, by Way of Jodoji,
and to Awaji

▦

The red sun of evening enveloped us. We were in the town of Ono, Hyogo prefecture. We had had to rush everything, including dinner, in order to be here just at this moment. It was no way to treat a guest all the way from Chicago. We hadn't had enough time to look closely at a previous construction site that deserved more attention, and were forced to satisfy our hunger with hamburgers eaten in the car on the way. But bathed in the evening sunset, we were quite happy. And Ando looked happiest of all; it had been very unlike him to push and rush his guests, but we now understood why.

It was in the autumn of 1982 that we met the Chicago architect Stanley Tigerman. He had participated, as had Ando, in a symposium on postmodernism held in Osaka. The symposium ended on Saturday, and the following day Ando invited Tigerman to visit the first-phase of his Rokko Housing project in the suburbs of Kobe. The site reverberated with the sound of concrete drills, not a place where one could stay for long, but still we donned helmets and clambered up and down ladders, in and out of scaffolding. Ando held forth with enthusiasm, but I could scarcely imagine how this mass of concrete would ever turn out to be a work of architecture.

During his explanations Ando danced about the scaffolding. Then suddenly he announced that the tour was over; we had to hurry to our next destination. It was afternoon when we left the site in the foothills of Mt. Rokko, and headed by car out of the city and over the mountains, nonstop through the countryside.

Finally Ando revealed our destination: "I thought I'd show our guest

Jodoji, Hyogo: view of Main Hall (twelfth century)

Jodoji." I could not grasp the reason Ando was so bent on taking Tiger-man to a remote, rural Buddhist temple like Jodoji.

"You can't show someone who's just arrived in Japan that kind of classical architecture and expect him to understand anything but the most superficial aspects," I thought.

Jodoji is a well-known building. Built by Chogen (1121-1206), it is a masterpiece of temple design and construction, as well as one of only a few structures remaining from pre-Kamakura period times. Chogen was a famous priest well versed in architecture and responsible for the advent of the new mode of building known as Daibutsuyo. This style dates from Chogen's rebuilding of the hall of the Great Buddha in Nara after it burned down in 1180. Jodoji and the South Gate at Todaiji are the most prominent extant examples of the Daibutsu style.

When you have a guest from abroad and want to show him classi-cal architecture, the normal procedure is to visit Kyoto or Nara. Last night, in Osaka, we had been closer to these two places than now, and the standard tour of the old capitals would have been quite possible. Yet Ando had chosen the out-of-the-way Jodoji for reasons of his own. The scene we were to witness was to be reincarnated as a new work by Ando nearly a decade later in a most curious way.

But let me return to my story. The ride after leaving the Rokko

Jodoji: interior of Main Hall

Housing site was rather tiresome. After we left the expressway, rural scenery stretched on and on, looking much like anywhere else in Japan. I kept thinking that Mr. Tigerman was being extremely patient.

Despite the rush and hurry, by the time the silhouette of Jodoji drew near beyond the rice fields, the sun was already close to the horizon. It was past the regular visiting hours, and we were almost turned back at the gate. But we couldn't simply let Tigerman go back to the United States after coming this far, and when we explained the situation, the people at the temple gladly reopened the main *hondo*.

As we entered the hall, we were met with a breathtaking scene. The interior was dyed scarlet in the setting sun. Directly ahead was the imperturbable figure of the Amida Buddha, and from behind it strong orange rays of the evening sun blazed through an open lattice, shining over the woodwork of the hall's interior and bathing the room in reddish light.

Buddhism teaches that the "pure land" (*jodo*)—or paradise—lies to the West. The scene that unfolded before us at Jodoji was a superbly magical moment inspired by that belief and dramatized architecturally.

Cloaked in the flood of the sun's rays, the presence of the Buddha gazing down upon us was overwhelming. One can easily imagine that farmers in the area, witnessing this scene when the temple was first built, could hardly have doubted the existence of a Pure Land whose rays shone so gloriously on their mundane lives.

Of course, the rays of the setting sun do not shine into the temple for long. It is a phenomenon that at most lasts twenty or thirty minutes a day. This experience of feeling the reality of the western paradise is possible only in the short moments when the sun, still barely above the horizon, stands framed in the latticework of the back window of the hall.

I was filled with admiration for Chogen, who was both a devout Buddhist and a brilliant architect. Inasmuch as it was Chogen who raised the funds required to rebuild the temple of the Great Buddha at Todaiji after its destruction in the wars between the Genji and the Heike, he must have been an extraordinary impresario. Look at his skill in staging this dramatic moment at Jodoji. It was more awe-inspiring than any contemporary effect one might achieve using all the lighting and sound effects of state-of-the-art technology.

I had witnessed striking examples of architecture as the handmaiden of religion in the cathedrals of Europe: Gothic spires that seemed to tower into the heavens, gigantic stained-glass windows, the echoing strains of pipe-organ music filling dimly lit naves. The impression was of the music of heaven pouring from overhead. There is no doubt of the Christians' power to dramatize such space for the benefit of medieval parishioners. Clearly such simple folk would have believed the cathedral to be under the control of some superhuman power. Such churches possess a truly calculated majesty, with their superb command of technology, dramatized by the builder's hand.

Yet it had never occurred to me that the dramatization of religious space was part of Japanese tradition until that evening at Jodoji. In this remote corner of the Japanese countryside Chogen built a temple filled with a splendor of religious majesty to rival any ever built in the West.

Tigerman was sitting motionless at the wall opposite the lattice through which the sunset streamed. He hardly moved. The glare must have been nearly blinding, but he gazed intently in the direction of the western sunlight, squinting slightly but barely blinking behind his glasses. The architect from Chicago was clearly taking in the scene bodily. Knowing that the light would last only a short time, he was concentrating every nerve on the experience.

As for me, I too gave myself up to the moment, so that later, as a critic, I could accurately reconstruct what I had experienced. Ando was satisfied. Even he, no doubt, had not experienced this phenomenon to quite such splendid effect.

Tigerman, a rival architect, and I had to be grateful for Ando's generosity in sharing with us this secret place. Had I been Ando, I might not have been able to overcome the psychological resistance to sharing an experience thus replete with inspiration. It was obvious that a rival could be nourished by the revelation it afforded. Such misgivings seem part of a deep-rooted envy shared by all artists. And such envy is inevitable, no matter whether the rival is from far away or close at hand. It was especially amazing to me then, at a time when Ando stood on the threshold of international acclaim. Yet Ando had even made Tigerman put up with considerable inconvenience and discomfort to bring him along on this trek.

The light lasted less than thirty minutes and then vanished, casting the hall rapidly into darkness as the sun sank in the West.

Each of us emitted a deep sigh. Reluctant to bid farewell to that "Pure Land of the West," we sat together in silence. All there were filled with a sense of gratitude toward Tadao Ando that was transformed into an absolute trust in him as an architect. This feeling, I believe, remains alive with those of us who experienced that precious moment.

It was a short trip, but I came to feel that Ando was something more than simply a talented architect. He was much larger. Much more than the Ando who was idolized in some quarters of society, this Ando seemed to have a mission to share his discoveries with others, regardless of who they were. That unforgettable autumn day marked the true beginning of my association with Tadao Ando and his career.

## Recollections of Rokko

Ten years after the evening at Jodoji, I was to have a second sudden and startling experience. But before I tell that story, I would like first to look back at how I later saw the completed Rokko Housing project, whose construction site Tigerman and I had toured.

I visited the completed first-phase of the Rokko complex with Ando one day in the summer of 1983. Ando was full of energy, running up and down the steps of the ten-story apartment block rising up the cliff, and expounded on his work with great verve. I was obliged to leave immediately afterward on newspaper business in Canada, but at the end of the summer I wrote a lengthy article for an architectural journal.

While reviewing the state of multiunit private housing in Japan at the time, I critiqued the Rokko Housing using "stairs" as a keyword and attempted to forecast the direction that Ando's work might soon take. I was still young and had just gotten my foot in the door as an architectural

Rokko Housing, Kobe: view of Phase I at completion ▶

Rokko Housing: bird-eye's view of terrace, Phase II

critic, and the spatial composition of the Rokko Housing complex held special appeal, as my article recalls:

"In the evening we used to hear people returning home, their footsteps coming up the staircase. Shoes were leather-soled then and made a squeaking sound as they came down on, and pushed off, the grainy concrete surface, each person making a distinctive sound. As a small child just having entered the world of conscious thought, it was easy to tell which sound belonged to my father, coming home to be with his family. Soon, listening for the sound that his shoes made became part of my daily routine.

"Of all my experiences of living in multiunit housing as a child, those relating to footsteps on the stairway remain perhaps the most vivid. In the latter part of the 1950s, my father, who worked for a shipbuilding company, moved out of his family's home with my mother and me to a three-story concrete housing complex owned by his firm. The apartment assigned us was on the top floor, and since two apartments faced each landing, it was the footsteps of six families that I listened to each day. Would the footsteps coming from the ground floor stop midway and end in the dull metallic sound of a regulation steel door opening, or would they continue upward? Would they stop at the door opposite ours or come to our own door?

"A child who is waiting to hear the sound of his father coming home has no complicated or ambiguous thoughts. It is simply a matter of making out the familiar sound of the footsteps and then feeling a sense of relief at having heard them. The footsteps made their way up to the third floor, and then the front door opened; that short interval of time was a great source of pleasure, something I looked forward to.

"From a different perspective, what did the mothers in the building think about this? Of course, they probably looked forward to the sound of their husbands climbing the stairs as much as their children, but they also felt a good deal of unease during the day, and also at night, at the approach of unfamiliar footsteps while their husbands were still away from home. It only took a couple of months after moving in to be able to tell which footsteps belonged to whom—whether they be the husbands, wives, or children sharing the building or regular delivery boys—and one's sensitivity grew rapidly after that. Thus, the sound of strange footsteps tended to be an increasing cause of worry for the mothers of the children living there.

"Habit can be a terrible thing. Through habituation, the layout of a

Rokko Housing: penthouse apartment, Phase II, and view of Kobe Harbor ▶

building can make residents as sensitive to the fall of a footstep as the inhabitants of a prison are to the approach of a warden. My family lived in that multiunit building for some ten years, becoming more and more atuned to the sounds around us; then we made our escape, so to speak, and moved into a modest home of our own. It took a while, but eventually we stopped paying undue attention to the sound of people passing in front of the house. After all, most of them simply went straight on past, without giving a thought to us. It was quite different from the past, when we knew that the footsteps of a stranger would without fail make their way to one or another of the six units in the building—like a game of Russian roulette in which there was a one-in-six chance of your apartment being the target of the stranger's approach. Now that I think back on it, it seems silly to subject oneself to that kind of stress.

"In any case, possibly because of this childhood experience, whenever I visit multiunit housing, the first thing I notice are the stairs. In high-rise apartment houses, they are usually overshadowed by an elevator hall. Many architects have worked ambitiously in the housing field, and architectural journals give quite a bit of space to the subject, but in my opinion there has been little real progress in the matter of stairways.

"Tadao Ando first told me about his Rokko Housing project, which was to be a landmark undertaking, just after the completion of the Koshino House for the noted fashion designer. Because of the precipitous terrain, the big construction companies refused to take it on lest a disaster occur. But Ando was aiming at a work that would make history in the domain of multiunit housing. His explanation was still fragmentary, but I could tell that he was embarking on the project with high hopes. So immense was his zest for this job that every time I set foot in his Osaka office, he would drag me to the site to take a look.

"Rokko Housing clings to a bluff not far from Rokko Station on the Hankyu commuter line in the eastern suburbs of Kobe. Typical of the area between Osaka and Kobe, the slope north of the tracks is a comfortable residential area. After leaving the somewhat jumbled district around the station, the streets are lined with middle-class, upscale dwellings, and then suddenly one comes to a sheer cliff. Ando's housing complex is ten stories high, firmly set into the steep terrain. Looking at the tiny plots of the homes on the less precipitous surrounding land, one can easily see why such a large site had remained empty. The building's walls are Ando-style exposed concrete. Designed to fit the 60° incline, the apartments are set back in stairstep fashion, and the overall

Rokko Housing: detail of circulation space ▶

structure is divided into an upper and lower *parti* by a courtyard situated roughly halfway up.

"Did Ando succeed in making this complex stand out among its kind throughout the world? I believe that he has created a standard not achieved heretofore, certainly in Japan. And I attribute that success to one factor: its *stairs*.

"Stairways. As I said, they are to me one of the most important components of a housing complex. Yet I never dreamed that Rokko Housing would have stairs as its main provision for circulation. It is ten stories high and backed against a cliff, so the conventional choice would have been an elevator. But Ando had discovered his own distinctive solution, whereby he placed the stairways boldly in the center of the building. The elevator is tucked unobtrusively to one side. This decision is what makes the building unique.

"Upon entering, you first mount a four-level flight of stairs located centrally between the projecting lower wings of the building, emerging in a courtyard that separates the lower and upper sections. Those headed for apartments below approach via paths or stairways leading down into each unit; those going to apartments above must continue to climb.

"It is these steps to the upper units that provide the highlight of the design. Between the courtyard and the topmost tenth floor are five landings which form a convex tier of balconies at the center of the complex. The pleasure of going up and down these steps is difficult to understand, as is often the case with Ando's works if you have not actually experienced them. The lower section comprises four floors and the upper section six. Ascending six floors is a task you'd rather avoid, but when you start to climb these particular stairs, you find that you have reached the top almost without effort. I climbed those stairs the first time with Stanley Tigerman when we visited the site midway through construction. And I distinctly remember watching how easily the somewhat short and stout Tigerman made it to the top, causing me to feel these stairs possessed a kind of curious power.

"What is this magic? From what I sensed, it is light. The balcony landings appear vertically aligned, but on plan they are gradually set back as they ascend. Thus, spiraling upward, you periodically emerge into the open air and natural light floods the stairwell. Most stairs are dark and enclosed, but at Rokko the landscape opens before you at each landing, relaxing and drawing you forward.

"As it turns out, coming down the stairs is even more exhilarating. The top-floor view is unsurpassed, stretching in panorama from Kobe port on the right, across the city and its suburbs, and extending toward Osaka on the left. Beyond are the island-dotted waters of the Inland Sea. Descending the steps, with their intermittent sallies beneath the sky, one can't help but feel that all is right with the world. The nightscape from the hills of Rokko is often referred to as a 'million-dollar view,' and seeing it from these stairs after dark does indeed leave one feeling somehow enriched.

"Another reason for the success of the stairs comes from Ando's attention to detail. It is said that stairs should be judged less by how easy they are to go up than how safe they are to descend. From that point of view Rokko Housing is probably unsurpassed, and this must be attributed to a meticulous search for optimal tread-and-riser dimensions. The turn within the semicircular landings, moreover, comes quite naturally with each step, and in such matters Ando is at his best. His triumph results not merely from placing the stairway in the center on the main approach, but from specific forms that make you unresistingly embrace the layout.

"Stairways in multiunit housing have usually been left to chance. They are narrow and dark, often dank, and usually not visible from inside the units. My association of such dwellings with prisoners listening for a warden's footsteps must be due to the fact that stairwells were mere areas separating one unit from another, little more than a necessity. In Rokko Housing, Ando overturned that logic, and by giving stairways special treatment has begun to reverse the warped psychology I harbored for so long.

"Since the Rokko stairwells are open, the sounds of people coming and going echo less loudly, and because the stairs wind back with staggered landings, people coming up or going down are easily seen from within the dwellings, helping both to promote intimacy among residents and to forestall unwelcome intruders. Also, the necessity for all residents to climb up at least as far as the fourth-floor courtyard in order to enter their homes helps increase their awareness of community. In such ways, I believe Rokko Housing has earned for itself a place in the history of collective housing in Japan.

"Rokko Housing is noteworthy not only for the originality of its stairs but also the quality of its interior spaces. There are few, if any, architects with Ando's highly developed sense of proportion for the spaces with which a single human being has contact. This is amply demonstrated at Rokko. Not only are the stairs of an appealing scale, but the relationships between depth, breadth, and height in each room are comfortable. Considering that the tiny Izutsu House in Osaka displays the same keen sense of proportions, we must conclude that Tadao Ando is at the top of his form."

After publication of this article from which I have quoted at length, the trip to Jodoji with Tigerman and Ando slipped into the realm of pleasant memories. Yet it was to be freshly evoked in the most unexpected way in 1993.

Rokko Housing: detail of flying concrete beam

# The Lotus Temple on Awaji

Ando and I met in Kobe and crossed over to Awaji Island by ferry. The night before I had stayed at a hotel over Osaka Station, my only choice after working late and leaving Tokyo on the last Shinkansen. So early next morning I took a semi-express of the now privatized Japan Railways as far as Kobe Station, where I met Ando. Together we took a taxi to the port at Takatori.

Located at the west end of Kobe harbor, Takatori is right across the Akashi Straits from Awaji. A half-hour's ferry ride would get us to the island for a look at Ando's latest work.

"Did you know that this ferry and all the buses on Awaji Island are run by the Iue family?" commented Ando.

"You mean the Iue of Sanyo fame?" I said. The famous Konosuke Matsushita, founder of Panasonic, had married Mumeno Iue; her younger brother Toshio, who worked for a time as Matsushita's right-hand man, later founded Sanyo Electric.

"Yes, that's the one. The family owns everything."

Our destination, the Honpukuji Mizu-mido or "Water Temple," is located on a small hill in Higashi-ura on the northeast tip of Awaji. Taking a taxi from the wharf and then walking, we reached the temple at the top of a short, steep hill.

Honpukuji had long been the family temple of the Iues, who come originally from Awaji and have not faltered in their support of it. Ando now enjoys the exceptional confidence of powerful Kansai area business leaders, and at his request they frequently vie to lend a helping hand in support of culture or volunteer relief. For instance, Ando has been a prime mover of the Osaka 21st Century Project for urban renewal since the 1980s. It was such ties that led Satoshi Iue, then president of Sanyo and the son of Toshio Iue, to ask Ando to design the Honpukuji "Water Temple," completed in 1991.

Ando had been talking to me about the scheme for several years, referring to it as the "Lotus Temple." He had devised a bold structural concept whereby the main body of the temple would be submerged, with the only visible feature a serene lotus pond.

Ando admits that he met resistance to this idea from other supporting families of the temple. It is easy to see why. To build the main image hall beneath a pond would court the risk of leakage, and besides, it was just too removed from the ancient typology of Buddhist temples, which calls for a certain grandeur and an imposing architectural pres-

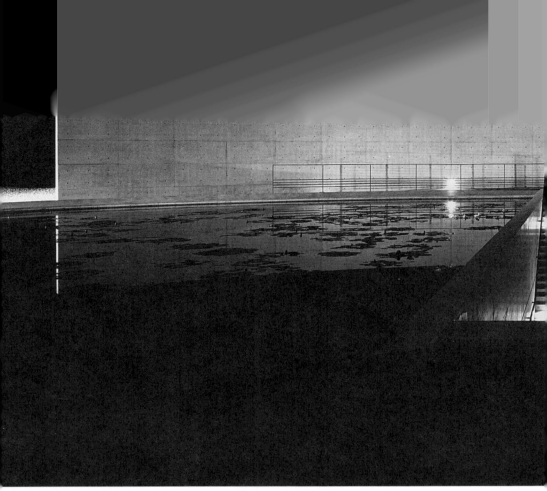

Honpukuji Water Temple, Awaji Island: view of lotus pond toward entrance

ence. The head of the Shingon sect, too, expressed skepticism, maintaining that, "The dignity of a Buddhist temple is displayed in its roof. We have our doubts about a temple building that doesn't even *have* a roof."

But with the powerful advocacy of Satoshi Iue, Ando was able to overcome all opposition. It is said that his victory was won by a reference to "the gratitude one would sense when entering the space beneath the lotus, symbol of the Buddha."

I was eager to see how he had realized this concept. As we drew near the site, the temple burial grounds spread out on either side, but there was nothing dark or dismal. It lay within the gentle landscape of trees and fields under the hazy light typical of the Inland Sea, and the view beyond its tombstones opened toward the sea. There was something free and clear about the continuity between this old cemetery and

the surrounding life of the town, unlike either the dark dankness of European graveyards or the bleak gloom common to Japanese cemeteries.

Already, from the highest point beyond the cemetery, we could see the "Water Temple." All that was initially visible was a flat wall. The entry was strewn with large white pebbles. The wall is typical Ando-style poured-in-place concrete, its dark gray alongside the bright pebbles engendering an air of solemnity. It was the embodiment of modernism's pared-down aesthetic.

You then walk between a straight and a curved wall. The space thus delimited forms the temple approach, purifying and preparing one for entrance into the inner sanctum. Suddenly the walls end, and before you is the round pond filled to the brim with dark green water. The

Honpukuji Water Temple: interior of main hall with Pure Land altar

pond, too, is framed in concrete. Two walls form a slit down the center, with a flight of stairs leading to the temple hall below.

Following the head priest, I descended the stairs and turned into the right-hand room. It was an assembly hall for members of the temple parish. Though underground, the room was bright with natural light. The building as a whole is a concrete cylinder with a roof-top pond, half submerged in the slope of the hill. The area of wall that projects from the slope has openings to bring in light, so the interior is nearly as bright and pleasant as any ordinary building.

The priest's explanation ended, we moved into the main image hall on the opposite side of the stairs. At the entrance we were met by a young student priest from Southeast Asia, and then we went inside.

What awaited us there was the reddish glow of ten years before.

The light was controlled here, too, by an immense oblong lattice, its mullions painted scarlet. Through this filter the light flooded across the room. It was tinted a subtle shade of red reflected from the gray concrete in an indescribable hue. This was the first time I had seen color introduced in any of Ando's works. Ando had hitherto pursued an ascetic art totally unrelated to color.

My first reaction was ecstatic. The color itself was splendid. Though I had been aware of Ando's pride in the work, I never thought to encounter such beauty. I believed his satisfaction was connected with the tour de force of building the hall beneath a lotus pond, and he had not said a word to me about the space. Now I could see why he had been so confident in anticipating my surprise, and I had stumbled headlong into his wry trap.

At first sight, I did not recollect when or where I had seen this color before. Then, as I passed through into the main image hall, the memory surged back upon me, and I became intoxicated with the historical dimension of the architect's conception.

A Budda image was enshrined in the hall. We had entered at an hour not very late in the afternoon, but the red of the setting sun already filled the hall. And then I knew. It was the blazing glory of the "Pure Land of the West" once more illuminating the figure of the Buddha. Beyond the altar of worship was a large lattice aperture, and as we stood facing the Buddha, a dazzling halo obscured all details of its expression or attire. From behind shone solemnly the merciful light of Paradise, a soft spreading glow bespeaking its blessings.

Here was a literal re-evocation of the space Chogen had brilliantly inaugurated at Jodoji. The aura of the ancient temple we had visited a

decade ago had been recreated eight-hundred years later. The usual approach to securing the grandeur of older religious architecture in the present is to reproduce the old forms in contemporary materials; but, with very few exceptions, such attempts always fail. There are countless examples in Japan of temples that have become cold and lifeless because their forms, once stately and graceful in wood, have simply been replicated in concrete. In the "Water Temple," Ando has demonstrated one important truth for achieving success in the building of temple architecture in concrete.

What must be passed down is not finite forms, but the quality of space itself. The essentials of Chogen's space, as we observed it that fall evening back in 1982, had clearly been etched on Ando's soul. He had tackled the ultimate challenge of an enthralling religious space, and here was his response. He had furthermore sought to make the phenomemon captured by Chogen into a more lasting effect. Chogen had designed Jodoji in such a way that it could achieve its greatest effect only during a limited time at evening. By contrast, Ando devised a way by which the "light of the Western Paradise" might be prolonged, and that was the reason for his bright red latticework.

Since the image hall at Honpukuji is set below grade, the flow of light to the interior is inevitably limited. Thus the design is contrived so that all the available light will be tinged with red. This way, even when there is no striking sunset, the "light of the Western Paradise" may still be experienced. Ando's resourcefulness has given the "Water Temple" one of the most elegant and refined conceptions of any contemporary religious building in Japan.

It hardly needs saying that in terms of originality and concept, architecture requires a long-term perspective. Attracted to architectural history, I have always believed that historical knowledge and perspective are crucial to any critique of the contemporary. From the time of Ando's plans for the renovation of the Osaka town hall and other buildings at Nakanoshima in the 1980s, he had begun to view the city in historical perspective. However, since I felt that the town hall should either be wholly preserved or else replicated, I was skeptical about the extent to which history really shaped Ando's vision as a contemporary architect.

After seeing the "Water Temple," however, I was amazed and touched to find that an architect's intuitive feeling for history can be unexpectedly strong and unerring. It was Ando's contemporary version of Jodo-ji, wrought in concrete. My first thought was to exclaim to Ando how I

◄ Honpukuji Water Temple: detail of wall curvature and lattice admired his building and to confirm its connection with our experience of so many years ago. Still, thinking he might find that tactless, I held my tongue and celebrated this splendid work in silence. Yet, I was sure I was right about Ando's tribute to Chogen in this work.

We left the temple and walked down the slope, returning to the wharf. There was a while to wait before the ferry back to Kobe came in.

"Shall we have a bowl of udon?" Ando offered in his usual unaffected Kansai drawl.

Still high from what I had seen, I finally came back to earth, "Let's do that."

We sat at the counter in a corner of one of the souvenir shops next to the pier, slurping our udon. We said nothing about the temple. We didn't have to, because we both knew what it represented and how splendid it was.

"Iue runs this place too, you know," was his irrelevant comment. The noodles were Ando's treat, and it was the best lunch I could remember in a long time.

# BLACK PHANTOM THEATER

## To Ikebukuro, Shinjuku, and Asakusa

▓▓▓

The opening of the Tadao Ando exhibition at Tokyo's Saison Museum of Art in Ikebukuro in June 1992 was a gala affair, with a great many toasts and speeches saluting the architect. In Japan events of this kind are usually dominated by people from the world of architecture, but this occasion was different. I was amazed at the number of guests from the fields of design and fashion, as well as the world of business. The gathering clearly reflected the immense depth and breadth of Ando's popularity and acquaintance.

Chatting in the exhibition hall with Ando's wife after the reception, I heard a well-modulated female voice call out in congratulation. Turning around, I recognized the smiling face and slender figure of the actress Li Reisen.

I was surprised, as well as relieved, to see her there. An incident had occurred four years earlier—and had troubled me ever since—concerning Ando's design for the Shitamachi Karaza theater. Her presence at this major retrospective of Ando's works meant that we could put the events of the past behind us.

The story goes back to an encounter one spring evening in 1987 in the precinct of Hanazono shrine in Shinjuku, in the red canvas tent of the Jokyo Gekijo (literally, Situation Theater) troupe led by Juro Kara, well-known playwright, director, and actor.

In the years leading up to the overheated "bubble" economy, Shinjuku was still a decidedly unsavory place. In particular, the stretch between City Hall avenue and the Furin building was one of the most notorious spots in Tokyo, where gangsters could be seen strutting around in broad daylight—an ideal place to taste some of the less humdrum aspects of city life.

Amid these unsavory surroundings lies the quiet precinct of the Hanazono shrine, where in those days the Situation Theater's red tent had become a local landmark. There Kara's troupe vigorously upheld the small-theater tradition of the avant garde, despite a recent upsurge of lighter productions like those of the Yume no Yuminsha and troupes of the post–student-movement era. Kara, its chief playwright, and Li Reisen, the Situation Theater's star, made a dynamic team. At the time, they were husband and wife.

That day, having received a call from the man in charge of production at the Situation Theater, I had set out for the Hanazono shrine. The heyday of the theater under Jinpachi Nezu was over, but under the energetic and creative direction of Kara, determinedly surrealistic performances such as *The Turn of the Screw* continued to be compelling. The production manager informed me that a project was underway for Ando to design a mobile theater and asked me to be present at the consultations. The collaboration of two such strong individuals as Kara and Ando promised to be exciting. If their plans came to fruition, it would result in something entirely new.

When I reached the tent at Hanazono shrine, the two men were already deep in discussion. The plan for the mobile theater Ando outlined was quite attractive. He proposed a structure composed entirely of the steel pipe used to erect construction scaffolding. The assembly instructions could be faxed to the site—wherever it might be. Scaffolding pipe is universally available, so in theory the theater could be assembled anyplace in the world, implying a mobility even greater than that afforded by a tent.

Kara was thoroughly in favor of Ando's proposal, fascinated by the idea of a theater that could materialize anywhere. I remember feeling then how spellbinding architecture can be. As it did with Adolf Hitler, architecture can engender all kinds of mental fantasies. I looked forward to seeing how Ando's theater would inspire Kara's future productions.

Ando took a small roll of paper out of his briefcase and showed it to us. It was a sketch of a theater done with a brush in *sumi*-ink on Japanese paper. The design reminded me of the so-called Black Crow donjon from Japanese history. The cylindrical body of the theater was surmounted by a conical roof. The entrance was a wide, half-moon-style bridge set about midway beneath the eaves.

I had hardly expected to find Ando experimenting with such Japanesque forms. In clarity and elegance, the sketch was very impressive. It would be interesting to see how Ando, who had always worked with modernist, geometrical forms, would handle a Japanese-style design— and not just of interest to me alone. I was convinced the design would cause quite a stir.

"Good idea, wouldn't you say?" said Ando. Kara and I had to agree. The main problem was to find a site. One suggestion was the area around Shinobazu Pond in Ueno, where the Situation Theater had once pitched its tent. Ando believed that local governments might be approached to offer vacant properties for temporary use. Another obstacle was how to defray construction costs, but since the main material would be mere pipe, we thought that could be handled with relative ease.

Later, on a warm pleasant May day, I met Kara at Ichigaya Station. The cherry trees along the old moat embankment were in full leaf and there was an early summer breeze. We were going to discuss building arrangements. Ando had been hard at work and the way was now open to begin. Construction costs were to be borne by the Saison Group headed by businessman and writer Seiji Tsutsumi. The design Ando had created was to be built first in Sendai as the Saison Pavilion for the Future of Tohoku Expo, opening there in summer. After being dismantled, the structure would be re-erected in Tokyo, utilizing drawings transmitted by fax.

As we strolled up the hill from the station, Kara was in high spirits. Yet he had heard that the Saison Pavilion at Sendai would house an exhibit of marine life: what would we do if the canvas covering stank of fish? Teasing him for his overconcern, I reassured him and we strode onward.

At the contractor's office, we were met by a number of staff and a model of the proposed building. When an architect is as well known as Tadao Ando, the construction company throws itself into the project, and we found that they had done extensive engineering studies prior to the meeting.

"Scaffolding is ordinarily secured partly by the building that is going up inside it," they advised, "so it won't be easy to raise scaffolding on its own."

Not having thought of this, I was a bit taken aback.

"Structurally, it will present problems. For example, you won't be able to suspend anything heavy from the structure."

"What about stage lights," was Kara's immediate question.

"Not even stage lights. They'd be too heavy."

"After the structure is dismantled," I wanted to know, "will a rebuilding be feasible?"

"The structure will require specially manufactured clamps designed with the aid of a computer. It's hard at this stage to tell whether these elements will be reusable after it is taken down."

Did that mean, I asked, that it could not, after all, be built just anywhere?

"We figure the cost of rebuilding the dismantled structure at roughly seventy percent of new construction. So you may want to build from scratch each time."

"After the expo, how can the materials be transported to Tokyo?" I asked.

"We calculate that the materials other than pipe will fill several dozen ten-ton trucks," they said. "You'll need a place to store it all."

This was not what we had expected. Kara and I had been reveling in tantalizing visions of a mobile theater. The tent was eminently mobile: it arrived in a town like a fresh wind, was set up, and performances began. Afterwards, it was taken down practically in a moment and disappeared like a passing breeze.

The tent venue for performances was inextricably tied to breaking with established concepts of orthodox theater, whether in the red tent of Kara's Situation Theater or in the black tent of Makoto Sato's company. It was crucial to Kara's concept that the theater itself be lightweight and mobile. We realized during our visit to the contractor that their understanding and ours did not always jibe.

I don't know what Kara himself was thinking that day. Certainly he must have realized something of the limitations of "architecture." It stands to reason that an architectural structure is harder to move around than a tent.

I wondered how Ando would handle the technical issues that the engineers had raised, but I was not overly concerned. After all, the design for the Sendai expo had been finalized as a pavilion for the Saison Group; its "metamorphosis" as a theater for Tokyo was as yet not certain.

For one thing, a site had yet to be acquired. The troupe wanted it to be somewhere in Tokyo's eastern Taito ward, but each possible site ultimately had to be discarded for one reason or another. A great deal of time had been spent on the project, but the chances of its realization were still fifty-fifty. There was every possibility that the "Black Crow" theater would end up a phantom.

When I left the meeting with the engineers, I still did not feel particularly disappointed or downcast. After all, the structure the three of us had envisioned in the red tent that day would be realized, fish exhibit or not. The question of re-erection could wait, I thought, until a site was decided upon.

## The Alchemy of Artists

The spring of the following year, I heard that the "Shitamachi Karaza" was about to be realized. In other words, the scheme for a mobile theater that Kara and Ando had hatched that day in the tent at Hanazono shrine was to be carried out. Taito ward, which was involved in a number of community projects aimed at reviving the vigor of Tokyo's old Shitamachi area, had come through with a vacant site on the edge of the Sumida River. Kara had at once embraced the idea of helping Shitamachi, the homeland of Japan's urban theater. The Shitamachi Karaza was both the name of the theater and the name of a new troupe he formed to perform in this structure designed by Ando.

Kara himself was slated to perform, along with such well-known actors and actresses as Mako Midori and Akira Emoto. Midori, of the Dai-nana Byoto ("Seventh Ward Troupe"), had already played the lead in an original script by Kara performed in a former porno movie theater in Asagaya. Emoto was very popular with his unique characterizations on the Tokyo Kandenchi stage. These were names that regular theatergoers recognized, so the performances would make news.

I visited the Karaza during construction several times with Ando. Under construction, it was an exotic sight, steel-scaffold tubing glittering in the sunshine. As one might expect from an architect with a sense of proportion like Ando's, even the bare-bones structure was quite beautiful as art. I was excited to think how the work would appear when complete. From all I could see, the project was moving smoothly, and I had several requests to discuss it in the media.

Three days before the opening, I again went to the Shitamachi Karaza, this time with the photographer Koichi Saito to document the completed building. As we left our taxi on the banks of the Sumida River, the immense black-paneled exterior with its red conical roof loomed above us. The broad half-moon bridge leading into the theater was also in place. My first impression was that, as far as architectural form was

Shitamachi Karaza, Asakusa (Tokyo): detail of moon bridge and entry

concerned, it was a great success. As we were about to enter the theater, we crossed paths with Kara, so I called out, "It really looks great." He grunted in reply, "What does?"

Kara had never been a moody person, so his response caught me off guard, and I found myself at a loss for words. After finishing up my work with Saito, I called Ando and asked what had happened between him and Kara.

"He's gone and ruined my building," grumbled Ando. Inquiring further, I learned that when rehearsals had begun, it turned out that the performers' voices didn't carry to the audience. So, in order to solve the acoustics problem, Kara had ordered a large cloth hung from the ceiling. Apparently this violated Ando's aesthetic.

Ando's architecture is based upon an aesthetic of bare structure, or framework, unadorned by extraneous elements. Indeed, he feels strongly that the addition of any appendage or attachment violates the fundamental principles of design. He naturally opposed hangings of any kind in the interior, even for the sake of performance.

Kara, of course, has his own aesthetic. In turn he protested that the red of Ando's roof was not the color he had expected. Ando's retort was, "So, go paint it yourself," and he had a bucket of paint delivered directly to Kara.

It hardly needs mentioning that artists, by nature, tend to be somewhat childlike. With the simple-mindedness of innocent children, they are able to create works of widespread appeal. Because of this creative role, society indulges their willfulness. But should two such "enfants terribles" clash in earnest, there is little a third party can do. I had no hope of reconciling Ando and Kara in the short time remaining before the first performance.

The day of the opening, Ando, Kara, and I were scheduled to participate in a symposium arranged by Kazuko Koike in her nearby Sagacho Exhibit Space in Koto ward. Following the symposium, we would accompany guests from the Sagacho venue to the performance at Shitamachi Karaza.

The majority of the audience at the symposium would be prominent cultural figures and supporters of Ando. Koike's program had been arranged to allow the visitors to take in an exhibition, concurrently opened at her gallery, entitled "Tadao Ando and the Shitamachi Karaza." The atmosphere behind the scenes, however, was tight-lipped. Personally, I felt trapped.

I couldn't allow Ando and Kara to quarrel openly in public, so I would have to figure out a way to conduct the discussion without a clash. I might be a suitable moderator, but if the two should opt for confrontation, there was little I could do to prevent the audience from noticing their rift. I could only hope they would return to their adult senses. After all, the dream both had nurtured and slaved over for years was on the verge of achievement. The job of moderator is delicate to begin with, but I have seldom climbed a podium with so little idea of what to expect.

While I can't comment on the outcome of the symposium itself, I distinctly remember that the atmosphere at Sagacho that afternoon was not particularly comfortable. When I steered the discussion in the direction of Ando and Kara, in general they simply responded to my promptings, with little real dialogue resulting. Somehow we managed to fill the allotted time. Afterwards Ando and I boarded a water bus at a nearby landing and were carried down to the Shitamachi Karaza. I sat opposite Ando, and next to him were Toichi Takenaka, president of Takenaka Corporation, and his wife.

Ando held forth eloquently about a scheme to re-erect the Shitamachi Karaza as a watercraft in New York, and hold performances while floating down the Hudson River. An adroit conversationalist, Takenaka kept Ando engaged in good-humored repartee that helped us all feel relaxed by the time we reached the Asakusa wharf.

There was some time left before the performance began. The theater stood in a rather isolated place, but we found a small coffee shop in the back streets. While we were having a light meal, the actor Emoto appeared looking for a quick bite to eat. He greeted us, but perhaps because it was so close to performance time, there was a hard look to his eyes. We could sense the tension felt by an actor facing opening night in a new theater, and it raised our expectations for the performance itself.

A little after seven in the evening, the first spotlight fell upon the stage in a new work, "Sasurai no Jenni" (Jenny the Gypsy). It was a spirited performance, with Kara pushing himself to the limits. He threw himself not only into his role but also into the ring of water that encircled the stage.

It was a cold day for early spring. A bone-chilling draft blew through the perforated metal plates at our feet as we sat on low benches in the audience. A woman near me contrived to keep herself warm by wrapping a newspaper around her legs.

But Kara, seemingly mindless of the cold or his drenched costume,

Shitamachi Karaza: bridge and signboard tower

offered a stunning performance. In terms of production theory, it was doubtful whether the play represented anything beyond Kara's experiments going back to the 1960s, but from around the middle of the play such questions ceased to matter, either to the audience or to the performers. The theater critics sitting around us, as vulnerable as any other Japanese to tears, were quite overwhelmed by simple, unpretentious emotion. Surrounded by pitch-black riverbank shadows and enveloped in the darkness of the theater, Kara's spirit blazed forth on the dimly lit stage.

After the two-hour play ended, the audience, perhaps in response to Kara's astounding efforts, or perhaps in self-congratulation for being present at this cooperative effort by two provocative artists, continued to applaud as the cast returned for one bow after another. Then, as people began to stand up to leave, Kara leapt from the edge of the stage to the aisle leading up through the audience. He was headed for the spot where Ando sat, far in the back.

Ando stood as Kara rushed up. They embraced, their faces full of emotion. The national television network cameras, there to tape the play, recorded the scene.

Standing near Ando, I watched in bewilderment. Having observed the tension between them over the past few days, I would never have believed such a moment possible. I couldn't help asking myself if they knew what they had subjected me to. It had been tricky getting through a round-table talk with these two prickly personalities just a few hours earlier, and here they were embracing! I could only conclude that they had made up out of sheer euphoria over the evening's successful performance.

It had never been expected that these performances, no matter how marvelous, would pay for themselves. Even by the broadest calculation, it would have required two months of sell-out performances, at an equivalent of some $30 per seat, to earn the several billion yen for the construction costs of the theater, let alone salaries and general running costs for the troupe. The whole project was a profoundly interesting experience, but obviously not the kind of venture that would pay. Indeed, finances were to be the source of many difficulties for the Shita-machi Karaza troupe.

The series of performances on the banks of the Sumida played to full houses and received high praise in the media. In that sense, at least, the enterprise would have to be called successful. But it was success at a high cost.

Not long after, we heard that Juro Kara and Li Reisen had divorced.

Moreover, the red tent that had been the symbol of an era had vanished and the Situation Theater dissolved. The whole matter left a somewhat bitter taste in my mouth. I wondered, in fact, if it had been the seductive spell of architecture that had set these events in motion.

## Harvest of Discord

Summer came and Li Reisen was appearing in an independently staged performance of "The Tigers of Bengal." This time the theater was a renovated factory in Koto ward. Not having seen Li perform for quite a while, I decided to go.

It was a spirited performance. "The Tigers of Bengal" was written by Kara, and Li performed with tremendous energy, completely overwhelming her audience. She received an enthusiastic ovation. I, too, was impressed and thought I might write a review, so after the final curtain came down I went backstage to see Li.

I had gotten involved in the Shitamachi Karaza project because of my acquaintance with Ando and Kara. Ever since theatrical activity had come to an end at the "Black Phantom" on the Sumida, I had been fretting over the matter. How had that experience led to the demise of the Situation Theater, which had risen to such heights during the previous two decades? I had noticed that Li was never present at the Shitamachi Karaza. Had this been deliberate? How had Li seen the whole Shitamachi Karaza adventure? I decided the time had come to ask her about these things point-blank.

Li's answers were clear. First of all, she remarked, she could not in the least understand why the Shitamachi Karaza performances had been carried out without first making sure that ends would meet. Who had been behind it all, she asked, making no attempt to hide her anger. In short, to assure full appreciation of Kara's talents, the performances had to be commercially viable. A play that did not even give the performers minimum wage, she declared, was out of the question.

The kind of theater Li was talking about hardly made big box-office sales. She was simply making the point that in order for a troupe to maintain high standards as leaders of the avant garde, it needs to be sufficiently self-supporting. I now began to understand the fierce energy that had sustained the Situation Theater for more than twenty years.

Around that time, I saw Kara at the opening symposium for the

Sanseido Hall in Shinjuku. It had been my proposal that the symposium feature Kara, the novelist Mariko Hayashi, and the literary scholar Toru Haga. I recall Kara remarking from the podium that he now rejected architecture, and I naturally thought that these remarks stemmed from bitterness over the Shitamachi Karaza. The symposium itself was a success, with a program that had pleased the audience, but Kara's condemnation of architecture had been less than welcome to my ears.

So when Li Reisen appeared at the Ando retrospective in Ikebukuro, I felt the burden of a less-than-happy past begin to lift. I was grateful for Li's simple generosity in the matter. At last I might begin to judge for myself what the Shitamachi Karaza project had represented.

Two artists of highly idiosyncratic and original talent came together in the arena of architecture to create Tokyo's Shitamachi Karaza, one of the most unusual experiments of the late 1980s. Both architect and playwright faced many obstacles, but they pursued their vision of creating a theater in a mobile edifice. Through persistence, patience, and significant investment of energy, they realized the project virtually unaltered—in itself an immense achievement.

Looking back on Ando and Kara's experiment as contrasted to some of the more frivolous extravagances of the "bubble" economy—and then again in the context of the sharp decline in cultural activity since its burst—I cannot help but recall that period, with nostalgia and a sort of envy, as a time when people had visions that were important enough to inspire passionate feelings.

The project was not equipped from the outset with any mechanism to perpetuate itself. Indeed, the need for such a system was never considered. Of course, in any cultural endeavor, nothing can be accomplished if you are overly conscious of costs. The Shitamachi Karaza represented a joint opportunity for Ando and Kara to move beyond what they had been before. This is why a critic like myself, along with many others, cooperated and applauded their work.

The Situation Theater, however, is gone forever. I have set down my impressions of the events that led to its disappearance mainly because its demise seems to have been achieved via the medium of architecture. I am curious to know what theater historians might say about the Shitamachi Karaza—what it meant and what it achieved.

# THE GREAT EARTHQUAKE
## From Tempozan to Kobe

::::

O n a Sunday late in January 1995 I reached the Osaka Bay waterfront at Tempozan. My goal was Ando's recently completed Suntory Museum, about which I had been asked to write for an architectural journal. But given the catastrophic earthquake that had jolted the Hanshin region from Kobe to Osaka ten days earlier —resulting in a death toll of more than 6,000 and untold destruction—I could scarcely concentrate on the task at hand. Yet the wintry skies stretched transparent and blue overhead, and Osaka Bay rippled below in calm reflection. Ando's beautiful and accomplished building was poised on the edge of the bay.

But the catastrophic earthquake had made a mockery of all static values, leaving the entire nation stunned. I cannot deny that I wanted to wrap up my tour and catch the ferry for Kobe at once.

I had talked with Ando about his Suntory Museum many times. The project had turned out to be an adventure in restoring to the local citizenry a site on the edge of Osaka Bay where the jurisdictions of several government authorities intertwined. Ando had spoken passionately of his determination to achieve a real breakthrough in waterfront development.

I knew why the topic stirred him so deeply. The Osaka port zone had long been the preserve of factories and other industrial facilities, but recently people had begun to call for free access to the waterfront. At the height of the overheated "bubble" economy in the late 1980s, properties along Osaka Bay were being gobbled up in a "waterfront boom" by commercial developers. In vetting his plans for the Suntory

Museum, a persistent Tadao Ando had prowled through Osaka municipal and corporate offices, arguing in favor of an open public space for recreation at the water's edge. His behavior was rooted, I felt, in the basic concern of an architect who conceives spaces that are essentially public.

In the wake of bubble-economy development fever, the existing Tempozan waterfront, at the mouth of the Aji River that runs through the city of Osaka, was changed beyond all recognition. Already in place was the large-shouldered Kaiyukan Aquarium designed by Cambridge Seven, the embodiment of the boom in commercial waterfront development that had touched many cities in the United States and around the world. The cultural sophistication of the Suntory Museum was expected to defuse crass consumerism in the area.

In order to review Ando's work, I had originally planned a trip to Tempozan on January 16th, the day before the quake, but had been unavoidably, and fatefully, detained by obligations in Tokyo. Like many, I felt almost guilty to have been left unscathed by the disaster while old friends and acquaintances had been driven from their homes and suffered loss of family. Moreover, countless hardships were to continue for months afterward. That morning, Ando in London and I in Tokyo immediately learned of the disaster that had struck the region of our birth and roots.

From the time the news broke, I was completely inundated by my responsibilities as a reporter. I was tied to my desk in Tokyo while with each passing hour reports came in about the safety or plight of friends and relatives. The destruction in the Kobe area was far greater than initially estimated and casualty figures kept rising.

Television reports of the devastation in the downtown sections of Kobe, Sannomiya, and Nagata were heart-rending. I could hardly believe the urban landscape I had grown up with was now buried in rubble. Ando immediately started for Japan upon hearing the news. The Hanshin area was the location of many of his buildings, which he felt responsible for.

On the night of the second day, my phone rang well after eleven. Somehow I knew it would be Ando.

"It's a mess! Kobe's badly hit." Even over the phone I could sense Ando's indignation and anger. He seemed to boil with fury at the quake, or rather at the cruel fate that had enveloped the city and its people. I readily shared his anger and bewilderment, as both of us had roots there, roots that transcended our occupations as architect and critic.

Why did the city that that formed our cultural bedrock have to fall victim to such tragedy?

"You've got to come and see for yourself," he said hoarsely. "It's far worse than on TV." I could discern a heartfelt entreaty. The following weekend I cleared up my work and took the last bullet train from Tokyo for Kyoto. The next morning I boarded an early train, eventually arriving at Tempozan.

As it happened, Tempozan, site of the Suntory Museum, was also one of the few points of departure by public transport for Kobe. Automobile traffic had been blocked when the Hanshin Expressway toppled, and other trunk routes connecting Osaka and Kobe were likewise destroyed. Special ferry transport had begun to ply between Tempozan and Kobe to deal with the emergency.

During our talk before I left Tokyo, Ando had asked me to write about the quake. He seemed to be saying the Suntory Museum was now a matter of secondary importance. But for Ando the museum was a turning point, and I am sure he was looking forward to my article on it. Listening to the way he spoke, I was deeply moved.

To be honest, I was unsure how I ought to respond to Ando's appeal. He had said to go and look at the devastation and to write about it, but I vacillated, wondering whether, all the same, I should concentrate on the Museum. Or should I, after all, give over the space allotted to my architectural review to a report on earthquake damage?

In the end I opted to follow Ando's suggestion. I did so believing that there were two overlapping issues here that might be extrapolated from the situation: the "public" issue that was a key theme of the Suntory Museum on the one hand, and the public irresponsibility of the city of Kobe even before disaster fell, on the other. The municipality—despite playing an excellent role in public housing—had succumbed to rabid commercialism that had long ago earned it the name "Kobe Inc."

When I at last reached Tempozan station, the place looked completely different from when I had attended the aquarium's opening back in the days of the "bubble." The excitement of that time was no more. Wondering where to catch the Kobe-bound ferry, I found no signs anywhere, and when I asked city employees on the pier, they couldn't tell me. Local people seemed sympathetic to Kobe's plight, but their public servants seemed somehow lacking.

First I did a quick tour of the Suntory Museum and then headed back to the wharf to find the ferry for Kobe's Harbor Land. But before I go further, I would like to record my impressions of the museum.

Suntory Museum, Osaka: art gallery with IMAX Theater behind

The Suntory Museum fronts Osaka Bay. It is not only outstanding as a work of architecture, but also an exemplar of how to make the most of a waterfront site. The harborscape of Osaka is a far cry from the romantic scenery of 100-year-old ports like Kobe, Nagasaki, or Hakodate, where attractive cities were laid out in the Meiji era between steep mountains and coasts blessed with deepwater channels. As a much older city, Osaka is today largely urban sprawl, and the industrial districts of the lower-lying areas of the city extend uninterrupted to the water's edge. Ando had earlier transformed a corner of the city of Kyoto with his three-phase commercial building "Times," facing the Takase River. Now in Osaka he had wrought a completely different landscape, upon an otherwise undistinguished stretch of bayfront, by insisting that the site for the Museum face the water.

Suntory Museum rises above a flight of steps stretching to the water's edge. Not intended for climbing up and down, they are more like the tiers of an amphitheater. But there is no stage, of course, nor are performances ever held. Rather, it is a place of relaxation, where visitors having toured the exhibits emerge in threes and fives, to sit and talk about what they have seen and experienced. The vista before them, hitherto confined to the Museum's halls, is shifted to a seemingly infinite horizon.

The Museum brings to mind two other scenes. One is the Cergy Pontoise metropolitan axis currently being extended by the Israeli architect Dani Karavan outside Paris. This project, in which the new town is laid along a three-kilometer urban axis, has met with considerable success, its buildings (many designed by the Catalan postmodernist Ricardo Bofill) conceived not as individual entities but integrated in the context of the landscape.

The other site is Battery Park City in New York. This new office district at the southern tip of Manhattan was undertaken in an ambitious collaboration between now defunct real estate developer Olympia and York and the distinguished New Haven-based architect Cesar Pelli. The appointment of top-notch landscape architects in the project is notable, affording people working in the area fine views of the Hudson River estuary and the ocean and making Battery Park a new downtown attraction.

Ando's Suntory Museum design has a good deal in common with the successful approach of these two projects. His generously proportioned amphitheater steps have their counterpart in the steps Karavan built down from the plateau overlooking the Öise River in an attempt to bring people into direct contact with the pastoral landscape once painted by the Impressionists. Similarly, the steps at Tempozan remind me of the exquisitely people-centered promenade along the Hudson, revealing the beauty of wind, water, and light to be found even in New York Harbor.

The columns with which Ando fronted these steps are of the same grand proportions as the twelve columns Karavan set up at Cergy Pontoise (replicating the measurements of the supports of the Arc du Carrousel at the Tuileries in Paris). Karavan's aesthetic, however, is a neoclassicism reminiscent of the sternly perfected forms of the 1930s that differs from the rather relaxed atmosphere of Battery Park.

Here, Ando's awareness of the public nature of waterfront space had made accessible to all what might have remained simply open, unfrequented land. To the bayside at Tempozan, to which the Kaiyukan Aquarium first brought a certain hustle and bustle, Suntory Museum adds a sophisticated asceticism. But I found my mind dwelling much less on how comfortable this place would be for art connoisseurs and romantically inclined young couples than on what I was certain to find across the bay in the wake of the Kobe tragedy. I was feeling restless and wanted to be off.

## Destruction of Memory's Landscape

I headed for the Tempozan wharf where the high-speed ferry departed for Kobe's Harbor Land. With so many other routes to the city shut off by the disaster, a long line of passengers had formed on the quay. They clutched emergency food and drinking water; everyone was dressed in the warmest of clothing, because heat was at a premium in the quake-devastated city in late January. It took a long time, but one by one the people filed into the boat, packing close together to make room. As the boat sped toward Kobe, I strained to catch sight of the familiar suburbs—Amagasaki, Nishinomiya, Ashiya—stretching between Osaka and the eastern edge of Kobe. From this distance, little seemed changed. It was hard to believe that a catastrophe had actually occurred.

But as we neared Rokko Island, which had been created off Kobe by landfill, we could see how the sea wall at the water's edge had cracked and slipped. As we reached Port Island, moreover, we noticed that the artificial underpinnings of the land were seriously damaged. Still, we were too far away to gauge the true extent of the damage.

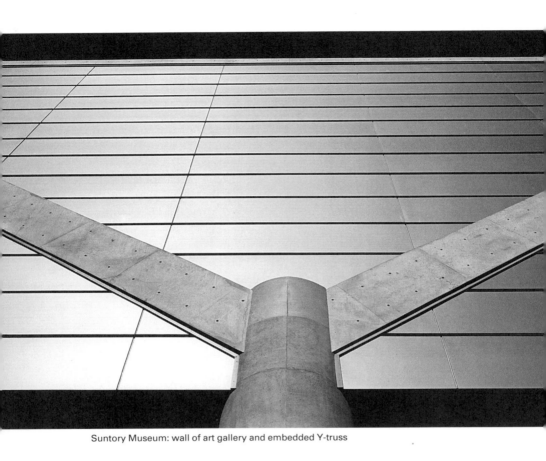

Suntory Museum: wall of art gallery and embedded Y-truss

Most of my fellow passengers were silent, many with eyes closed. They were obviously exhausted from traveling back and forth with supplies for friends and family, or absorbed in thought about the uncertainty of the future on their way back from visiting relatives in Osaka to get a much-needed bath. And there I was looking about with an eagle eye at every little detail. I suddenly felt ashamed of myself and oddly out of place.

Disembarking at Harbor Land, we saw volunteers distributing bread and sweet rolls and almost everyone accepting what was offered. There were lines at the portable latrines set up along the quay.

I set out for Kaigan Dori, the harborside location of many of the now historic buildings that had been landmarks of the city since the port was opened to the West in the mid-nineteenth century. The terracotta ornament of the Kobe branch of the former Osaka Shosen Kaisha (OSK) shipping company designed by Setsu Watanabe had chipped off here and there and the mortar was cracked; it reminded me of pictures I had seen of the damaged Tokyo Kaikan on the edge of the Imperial moat in Tokyo following the Great Kanto Earthquake of 1923. Part of the brick tile on the former Daiichi Bank's Kobe Branch building designed by Kingo Tatsuno had cracked and fallen, vivid evidence of the quake's fearsome energy.

Most pitiful of all, however, was the former Mitsui Bank's Kobe Branch designed by Uheiji Nagano. It had been reduced to rubble. From around the corner of a partially surviving wall, a small bulldozer scuttled in and out, busily clearing away stone and broken concrete. This building had been, no less than the OSK structure, one of Kobe's oldest landmarks; now the once-majestic Ionic columns gracing its portals had disappeared without a trace. I was assailed by a sense of powerlessness, to think how nature had reduced this place—a bustling port city for more than a century—to ashes and rubble in one stroke. I was also taken aback at the speed with which the clean-up was going on. Even Ando remarked about it in a lecture he gave after the quake: "Japan is always so *efficient*. Too efficient. Architecture belongs to the public realm. Should the remnants of surviving buildings be torn down and cleared away as simply as that?"

The loss of these older buildings was a blow. It had been my encounter with the architectural heritage along Kaigan Dori that led me to become an architectural critic. I had been fascinated by the tales of that period, such as how the huge granite pillars of the Mitsui Bank had been worked at the seashore in Kobe at the time of construction. I had

Suntory Museum: night view

also been captivated at the sight of a small cluster of shops called Rose Garden, one of Ando's first works, which stands amid the clutch of Western-style structures in Kitano-machi off Kaigan Dori, and compares quite favorably with these historic buildings. Kobe was not only the city of my roots but also the force that destined me for architecture and led me to cross paths with Tadao Ando.

All the buildings along Kaigan Dori had suffered heart-rending damage. But as I moved from this street, no longer in the central part of town, to the newer thoroughfares of the contemporary city, it was obvious that this was a mere beginning; what I now witnessed was far worse. Office and commercial buildings erected in the 1970s and 1980s had collapsed, and in the worst instances they were beyond recognition, like the Daiei supermarket. Seeing the ruins of stores where I had often shopped took my breath away.

I walked on through the devastated city center, and drawn by the need to discover the fate of the suburb where I was born and raised, trudged eastward toward Ashiya. From Osaka, the JR main line was running westbound trains only as far as Ashiya itself, so the only way to survey the damage between Kobe east to Ashiya was to walk. As the crow flies, the distance from Harbor Land is fifteen kilometers, so I estimated that it would take at least four hours.

Ultimately I did not have the time or energy to see Ando's buildings. Passing out of the commercial hub of the city and into the suburbs, I encountered even worse destruction. Vulnerable frame dwellings had been reduced to piles of splintered timber. Bedding and scattered books were visible among piles of roof tile and broken timbers, vivid testimony to the drastic change from peaceful daily routine to disaster. A number of pilotis-supported condominiums built over ground-floor parking had buckled at the knees.

By the time I had traversed Fukiai, by the Rokko road, passed through Mikage and reached Ashiya, it was dark. My feelings of anguish had reached a peak as I found myself in front of a familiar camera store called Kanbei Hanaya, which was located along the main Hanshin national highway not far from the Ashiya River.

Kanbei Hanaya was what they called a *shinko shashinka*, one of the advanced "modern" photographers active for a half century prior to World War II. If you research the history of artistic movements in Japan from before the war, you often come across this word "shinko." Such "modern" photographers made a speciality of streamlined views and poses, just as modernist architects were devotees of geometry. Kanbei

Hanaya produced bold photographs in the style of Bauhaus-movement leader Moholy-Nagy and was among the first to absorb and disseminate the influences of modernism.

Hanaya ran this camera shop for a long time and was well known as a Leica dealer. The large, two-story wooden building near the Ashiya River was the base of his activity. I found this landmark literally cut off at the knees, its large, once-elegant gable roof fallen to one side. As I stood there, I felt that I was witnessing the destruction of one of my principle points of pride—modernism itself.

With its international ports of call and constant overseas contact, the Kansai area was always progressive and cosmopolitan; it was the first to receive the baptism of the Modern Movement in the 1920s. Japan's modernism blossomed in the Kansai area under the leadership of distinguished Secessionists like Keiichi Morita, along with Setsu Watanabe, Heizo So, Yo Miura, and Takeo Yasui. Behind their achievements was the strong support of Sumitomo and other Kansai-based business conglomerates.

I, and I am sure Ando, too, take great pride in this rich heritage of modern Kansai culture. We like to think that it is only upstart unsophisticates who *force* themselves to enjoy abstract art because it is the thing to do. Only those who have breathed the air of true modernism from their childhood, as it existed in Kansai even before the war, can really appreciate the modern aesthetic.

When I went with Ando to see the Izutsu House in Osaka, built for a woman who had long run a successful *okonomiyaki* restaurant, I have a clear recollection of him remarking on the unique sophistication and distinctive taste of the local people.

The destruction of the Kanbei Hanaya shop hit me hard. I was stunned to see the headquarters of Kansai's leader of modern photography thus hopelessly broken and twisted. I began to fear that the quake had not only wreaked widespread physical havoc on the city but also destroyed the milieu that had fostered modernism.

At the same time, the scene I had earlier viewed at Tempozan began to seem like an eerie illusion. I am not one to dwell on the past, but as a person closely involved in thinking about architecture and the city, I questioned the meaning of all our debates and discussions up to now. I had never really been in favor of the grandiose urban development policies of the city of Kobe and had warned of excess. My critique, however, had been aimed from a distance. Sparked by the apparent success of the Portopia and Urban Resort Fair schemes, developments on Port

Sunset from Mermaid Plaza ▶

Island and Rokko Island had forged ahead. And while the city poured funds into such projects, redevelopment of the old, densely crowded sections of Nagata and Fukiai was relegated to a back burner. It was these areas of Kobe that suffered the greatest devastation and the highest toll in human lives.

There are certainly good things to be said about the recent transfer of central authority that makes it possible for local governments to engage in more flexible urban planning. But who is going to bring them to task when cities concentrate resources in flashy national-scale projects along the waterfront while neglecting the more ordinary, routine work of inner-city maintenance that is one of local government's fundamental responsibilities?

When I finally managed to reach Ashiya Station, I was completely done in. I caught the train back to Osaka and changed for a late-evening bullet express bound for Tokyo.

Disturbed by a galling sense of loss, both for the seminal monuments of Japanese modernism and for my place of birth, I was unable to sleep a wink despite being totally exhausted. Nor could I bring myself to face my computer and get started on the Suntory Museum article.

## A City Regreened

The following day Ando rang. When I told him I had walked from Kobe to Ashiya, he was amazed. I spoke of my grief at our lost heritage and my irritation at the price paid for setting priority on profit in place of public responsibility. He was in total agreement. Rescue and emergency help for the quake-hit city had been delayed at both the local and national levels, so the ire we two felt was not aimed solely at fate and nature's brutal force. "People in Tokyo have no idea what has happened," he reiterated bitterly. He then told me about the inspection tour of his buildings that he had made with his staff. The good news was that nearly all of Ando's works had emerged undamaged. Moreover, the pool at Rokko Housing had been useful as a source of water for people nearby; on Awaji Island, where damage was extensive, the water in the pond atop the Honpukuji chapel turned out to be a boon to local residents.

After the Great Kanto Earthquake of 1923 in Tokyo, reconstruction had centered on housing and the many lightweight commercial struc-

◀ Suntory Museum: harbor traffic alongside Mermaid Plaza

tures of an Art-Déco character that rose defiantly on the city's main streets from Ginza to Kanda. But following the Hanshin earthquake, with the Japanese economy shaky after the recent collapse of the bubble, we could hardly hope for a new, more open townscape for the devastated center city of Kobe. Still, comparing the two disasters (in the case of the earlier Tokyo quake, much of the destruction was caused by secondary fires), the damage directly inflicted by the earth's movement was significantly greater in Kobe. This fact seemed to focus citizens' attention squarely on the role of architects and urban planners and administrators.

Probably out of his awareness of this adverse reaction, Tadao Ando launched and continues to lead a movement called the "Green Hyogo Network," aimed at tree-planting in Kobe, Nishinomiya, and Hanshin suburbs. A year after the disaster, cleanup and rebuilding had made rapid progress in Kobe's central shopping and business districts, but in outlying residential areas there were quite a few places where the land still stood vacant after the destroyed buildings had been cleared away. Ando made an appeal for support in planting trees that would blossom in white the following spring, both to regreen the city and to honor the memory of those who had lost their lives.

Many other prominent persons joined Ando in the Green Hyogo Network, including the philosopher Takeshi Umehara, Nobel prize-winning immunologist Susumu Tonegawa, and writer Jakucho Setouchi. With the funds obtained, they set up a system for purchasing trees to be planted both in private gardens and on streets in devastated areas. A pamphlet set the basic donation at ¥10,000, but from individuals Ando asks for as little as ¥5,000, or about $50.

The goal is to plant 250,000 trees in the rebuilt metropolitan area. People who want to plant on their own property may contact the Network and receive an appropriate tree or trees. They are asked to sign a pledge promising to take proper care of the trees, thus assuring that the donations to the Network are not made in vain.

As to why he backed this tree-planting movement, Ando explained that when you talk about "architecture" at a reconstruction site, vested interests invariably come into play and make it difficult to reach agreement. He had found, however, that when it comes to greenery, no one has any complaints. And Ando believes that one should start where one can.

It was about half a year later that I heard of Ando's plans for quake-recovery housing in a harbor-front area formerly filled with small facto-

Rose Garden, Kobe: façade

ries. The project was privately initiated and not necessarily coordinated with the activities of the official Kobe Reconstruction Council. A complex of fourteen-story apartment towers is now rising on the site.

In time Ando became actively involved in various activities relating to the aftermath of the disaster, such as an educational trust fund for orphaned children. The Green Hyogo Network was one of these efforts.

A little more than a year after the quake, Ando and I visited Kobe just as the first signs of spring were appearing. We called on the owners and managers of Rose Garden, Rin's Gallery, and other properties in the Kitano-machi neighborhood, asking them to participate in the Network. Five hundred Network-provided trees had been planted throughout Kitano-machi, and street maps now marked their location. A type of magnolia (*kobushi*) could be seen in the gardens of some buildings. Ando gazed at them pensively. In conjunction with this movement, he had recently called on the governors of the individual prefectures, asking them to contribute trees and plants for newly built parks.

At lectures and various other occasions, Ando continues to call for contributions to the Green Hyogo Network, large or small. He is especially enthusiastic about the Network because it provides a means of helping Kobe and the Hanshin area for those individuals who wish to do so. In fact, there are plenty of people like myself, natives of Kansai, who want badly to help in some way, but are tied down by commitments at a distance from the city itself. Ando appeals to people like us, who want to make a contribution but are perhaps reluctant to hand over a donation without any sense of how it will be used. That's why the easily understood concept of "¥5,000 for a tree" has caught on among Kansai migrants to the Tokyo area. The response to Ando's call has been very positive, helping the Network reach its eventual goal of 250,000 trees if the present pace is maintained.

Part of the reconstruction after the Great Kanto Earthquake of more than seventy years ago was the building of small parks adjacent to primary schools throughout Tokyo, which might serve as disaster refuge areas. The greenery of these small parks, limited though it is, has considerably enhanced the urban environment of the capital, which was led by the Imperial Capital Reconstruction Program. We can only hope that Ando's projects for urban rehabilitation, fueled though they are by the enthusiasm of one individual, will play a similarly useful role in breathing life back into the devastated city of Kobe.

# Ando in Current Perspective: Twenty Works

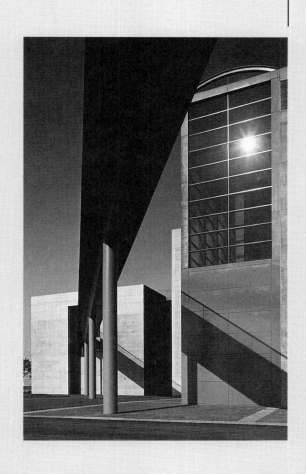

# CONTEXT

▦

Architecture creates an essential incongruity in the environment, stemming from the architect's urge to share the shapes of his or her imagination with others. Yet, quite often that urge is so idiosyncratic that it is unable to evoke any lasting response.

Architects have to face up to this incongruity, whether they be wanton ravagers of the environment or more restrained perpetrators of the same crime. The worst simply take it for granted that their creations will sooner or later be appreciated, no matter how ill conceived. After the first few favorably disposed clients, however, such architects may abruptly find themselves out of work.

What about Tadao Ando? His characteristic concrete, box-like forms do not, in a sense, appeal to popular tastes. Among his supporters are many who firmly believe in the twentieth-century myth that modernism's austere aesthetic is the natural style of an elite. Had modernist austerity been all Ando offered, however, his clientele would have dried up long ago. That his practice has flourished ever more vigorously over the past two decades suggests that his architecture has a more important role to play. I confess that I myself did not entirely recognize this special quality until the present decade.

One of the secrets of Ando's success can be seen in his "landscape-conscious" works that began toward the end of the 1980s. Starting with Raika Group Headquarters Building (1989) in Osaka and followed by the Children's Museum, Hyogo (1989), Garden of Fine Arts (1990) in Osaka, Kumamoto Prefectural Forest of Tombs Museum (1994), Osaka Prefectural Chikatsu-Asuka Historical Museum (1994), and continued most recently by Naoshima Contemporary Art Museum (1992 and 1995), Ando has set before us in clearest form the principles that inspire his architecture.

The key concepts are "natural environment" and "public building," and the perspective that shapes the works is best summed up as an "orientation to the landscape." This accentuates the public nature of all these buildings, and has led critics to praise not only Ando's unique aesthetic but also his truly landmark achievements in the public domain.

Ando's perception of landscape is two-faceted. He is aware of the incongruity of building in a landscape but also realizes that by limiting the building as something to be "seen," architecture may function as an apparatus from which to "see" the landscape. Landscape is thus accorded higher value than architecture, which becomes part of the landscape—embraced within it.

It goes without saying that architecture can be used to create landscape anew, but doing this well is difficult, except by constructing a "new town" on a previously undeveloped site. Ando's restrained expression in form-finished concrete offers the viewer an assurance that the work will not do the landscape any harm. His concrete boxes do not foist incongruity upon us as did the so-called Brutalism of the 1950s, which declared that rough-finished concrete represented the totality of twentieth-century expression.

Ando's restraint is most effective in these new "landscape-conscious" works of the 1990s. A simple concrete form against a backdrop of smooth green lawn in a sunshine-filled setting creates a wonderfully harmonious relationship between the natural and the artificial, discreetly impressing the viewer with all the finest qualities of twentieth-century architecture. Ando goes on to make this architecture an ideal device for viewing the surrounding landscape by skillfully adjusting the view from within the building.

In the antimodernist wave of the 1980s, the architects we lionized tried to resurrect historical expression—or experimented with bright colors and clever decoration—in an attempt to re-enliven cityscapes caught in the dour grip of modernist functionalism. They drew momentum from the simplistic bubble-economy notion that if office buildings and leisure facilities were constructed, jobs would be created and people would congregate. It was only a matter of time before the flaws of such beliefs were exposed. Indeed, when the bubble burst, society turned a cold shoulder on such opportunists for despoiling and cheapening the landscape.

Something had to be done to remove the unfortunate label attached to architects for spoiling the environment during the bubble when speculative private investment was at its height. Confidence in the architectural profession needed to be restored. One key to this lay in architecture's public nature. Ando's works have won increasing recognition for their awareness that landscape is a public asset.

In the recent boom, private corporations were even permitted to coopt and develop publicly owned land in ways that sometimes irrevocably transformed the landscape, most notably in waterfront development projects around the world. Ando's approach, which begins with his appreciation of and respect for existing landscape, offers remedies for some of the mistakes that were made.

# Raika Group Headquarters Building

If a landscape is to be presented to view, it ought to be presented in as attractive and beautiful a way as possible. This seems to be the thought that guided Ando in his design for the Raika Group Headquarters Building. In any particular project, the architect considers what can possibly be done to achieve its thematic aim. Ando's stated objective in the Raika building was to "control the look of the landscape from within the building."

Built for an apparel maker in a redeveloped industrial area on the edge of Osaka Bay, these offices were completed in 1989. The timing and location might lead one to suspect that the project owed something to the bubble economy, but Ando is not one to pander to the times. From the outset I imagined that he would be unable to follow the easy path of many of his contemporaries, and indeed the Raika building proved to be an advance in Ando's pursuit of an optimal relationship between architecture and environment.

Many saw the work as marking a turning point in Ando's career, as a move away from small- and medium-sized concrete dwellings in built-up urban areas to large-scale structures in more open settings. Indeed, this not inconsiderable concrete volume, rising on a relatively spacious site at Osaka Bay, is a rarity among Ando's works in that it can be viewed from all four sides.

Walking into the office space from the entrance hall, with its distinctive glass-block enclosed atrium, I began to appreciate Ando's

Raika Building, Osaka: main façade ▶

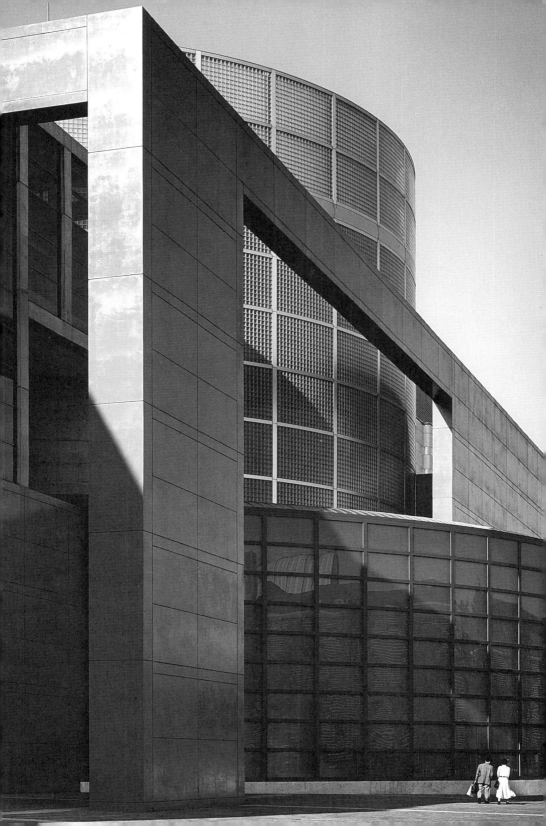

Raika Building: atrium and ramp

restraint as opposed to the atmosphere of "cheap chic" customary in such buildings, not to mention the typical heavy-cosmetic look so many offices had in the bubble era. But the biggest discovery was yet to come. When I looked out from the upstairs conference room, I realized I had come upon the work's essential theme. The only thing to be seen beyond the large panes of glass was a broad expanse of blue sky.

What had Ando achieved? By the simple device of setting a trimmed swath of roof garden on the terrace outside the glazed walls, he had contrived to create a landscape—to the viewer's eye, a framed portrait of light, wind, and sky—which is the best and most characteristic landscape the bayside area can offer. Tadao Ando has a distinct talent for perceiving the essential beauty of a particular landscape, and this bayshore zone was an ideal site. In the Raika building, for the benefit of those who must endure tedious executive meetings or sales conferences, Ando had become a landscape painter.

The roof garden device is simple enough, but without it one would be forced to gaze at the jumbled disarray of the waterfront itself, certainly more irritating than inspiring. The term "waterfront" makes it sound good, but the cityscape here, at the terminus of a new light rail line, is not an attractive sight. The mostly shabby, or at least far from spic-and-span, port facilities and tightly packed rows of municipal housing are rational but discordant. By any standard, the helter-skelter of warehouses, depots, and miscellaneous structures is dismal. Ando obliterated this hodge-podge in favor of a panorama of bright sky and sea breezes.

After this revelation, Ando's choice of glass block for the walls of the vast cylindrical atrium below becomes more comprehensible. Even nearby objects just on the other side of the wall are visible only in distorted outline; colors, too, are barely distinguishable. Yet, of course, ample light penetrates. In other words, here, as well, Ando is controlling the view. By means of the glass block, he shuts out the unattractive immediate surroundings, allowing only light and muted colors to enter.

The Raika building naturally comprises numerous details showing Ando's faultless sense of proportion, unnecessary to expound on here. More essentially, while so many architects working in the frenzy of the bubble economy were splurging on expensive materials and decorative frills, Ando alone opted for blue skies.

This is the kind of intelligence, signaling a refusal to be diminished by vulgar trends of the times, that we hope for in an architect. Following the light courts he created for the Sumiyoshi Row House in 1976,

Raika Building: studio space ▶

Raika Building: roof garden with view toward Osaka Bay

essentially his debut work in Osaka, Ando has here upheld his commitment to revealing nature in the midst of the city. I salute the brilliance with which he has deployed this affinity for nature once again in the Raika building. He stresses changeless priorities and enduring social values—unaffected by fickle trends of the times—and has managed to advance social and aesthetic aims in such a way that the client can accept and support them.

## Children's Museum, Hyogo

Each visitor to the Children's Museum, Hyogo, faces a walk of several hundred yards through the grounds. The walk would be shorter if you could park your car at the front gate and walk directly in through the courtyard, but that option is excluded. If you arrive from the city center, you find yourself near the main building, but must bypass it, completing a circle to the back of the grounds. Then you climb a steep path and make your way via a long, determinedly leisurely approach.

This approach is backed by a twenty-foot retaining wall of form-finished concrete that is Ando's trademark, with concrete underfoot as well. So one walks in obedience to the architect's commands, attention focused on the rounded forms of the Kansai landscape, cradle of Japanese culture. Ando's pathway is cut into the hillside, etched into the landscape like a Lucio Fontana work.

Ando's slash into the terrain seems intended deliberately to focus the visitor's attention on nature. On the right a panorama of gentle ridges peculiar to this western part of Honshu that faces the Inland Sea extends above a reservoir of algae-covered water. The architect has decreed that since you have come to visit this mountaneous museum, you should have some communion with nature.

Visitors are families, above all, who come by either bus or car. The natural environment of the museum is not particularly remarkable, but the architect has intended each visitor to listen and look while walking, in the hope that busy city dwellers will make this an opportunity to sense something precious that they might have otherwise forgotten.

All you need to do is walk. By gazing beyond the reservoir at the wooded, undulating hills, you find yourself reawakening to natural sights and sounds. Adults find city-dulled sensibilities revive to the feel of the wind, the smell of flowers and grass, and the warmth of sun-

Children's Museum: site plan

Children's Museum: panoramic view with museum at right

shine. Children feel a deep-down receptivity to nature well forth, possibly for the first time. And what could be better than for these newly aroused feelings to spark conversation between parent and child?

Here is a bold architectural technique one can admire. Having first gained recognition as creator of an "inner microcosm" in poured concrete, Ando here addresses the question of how people should be brought into this little world.

About a third of the distance along the path to the Children's Museum is a lookout plaza featuring sixteen square-sectioned columns. The solemnity of these geometrical forms characterizes Ando's restraint in interposing the artificial in the all-embracing landscape. Even more than with wall and walkway, we cannot fail to observe the architect's determination that such objects of artifice must be worthy of their natural setting.

This, surely, must be almost a gesture of invocation. Only after the architect has performed purificatory measures is he permitted to set alien forms upon the landscape. This realization somehow transmits itself to us who pass along this route, making us focus our attention. By the time we reach the main building, we are filled with a new alertness to our surroundings.

This atmosphere, with its solemnity and formality, was lost in public architecture of the 1980s, swept away by governments attempting to entertain and divert their citizenry. Such pampering, better suited to commercial theme parks expected to provide an experience worthy of the admission they charge, is grossly misplaced in a public institution. In eschewing this pose, Ando is not just bucking the current trend. On the contrary, he has determined the overall layout based on a careful study of what the users—say, of a children's center—require and expect of a particular building.

The natural environment of the Children's Museum is kept respectfully within view even from inside the building. As in the Raika Headquarters at Osaka's South Port area, these views are superbly composed. In the composition of an artificial landscape with a pond set at the end of the long approach path, we surely see the result of Ando's intuitive grasp of the potential relation between environment and function. With the Children's Museum, Hyogo, Ando redirected himself toward "landscape-conscious architecture" in a very positive and fascinating way.

Children's Museum: reflecting pool ▶

# Garden of Fine Arts

Expos and fairs have always held special attraction for architects. Ever since the Crystal Palace, designed by Joseph Paxton for the 1851 Great Exhibition in London, the world's very first international fair, such events have provided the ideal stage for architects to experiment with the most up-to-date techniques and materials.

By the beginning of the present decade, however, with the Osaka Flower Expo '90, the thread of this experimental tradition seemed lost. This was already clear at the Tsukuba Science Expo '85, held north of Tokyo. Architecture there was reduced to little more than shed-like structures housing mainly visual exhibits, and people had ceased to expect such fairs to suggest the future of architecture.

But Ando's pavilion, built for a game machine manufacturer and known as the Garden of Fine Arts, stood out among the rest of the buildings at Osaka Flower Expo '90. In representing a return to the original intent of such expositions, it diverged completely from other structures at the fair and was widely acclaimed.

The only strictly architectural element in the Garden of Fine Arts was a configuration of forty-five columns. Other than that, full-size

Garden of Fine Arts: with Michelangelo's *Last Judgment*

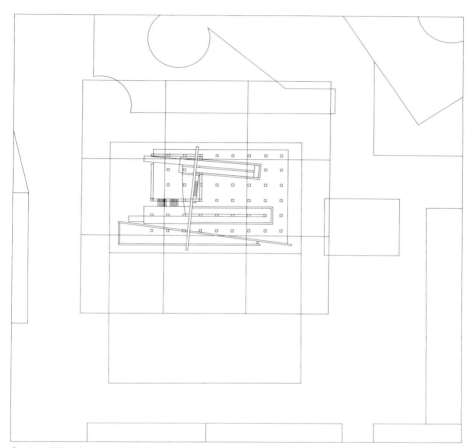

Garden of Fine Arts: site plan

Garden of Fine Arts, Osaka: general view

reproductions of works by Michelangelo (notably a vast replica of the *Last Judgment*) and other painters were reproduced on weatherproof ceramic tile; without Ando's fine architectural touch, they might have appeared as pure kitsch. Ando had dared to forego a building; as its name implies, what he made was a garden.

At ground level was a partially flooded concrete slab punctuated by regular rows of square-sectioned concrete pillars over forty-three feet high, with raised walkways, arranged to guide visitors along the exhibition's course. This device brought visitors face to face with the replicas of all these masterpieces in a stroll-garden context—and in the presence of water, wind, and light.

For me this garden was the most attractive feature of the Expo. Strolling through the other corporate-sponsored pavilions, sweltering in the summer's heat intensified by vast expanses of asphalt, I wondered how anyone could call the show a "garden and greenery expo." The majority of these pavilions followed the fashion for computerized exhibits and were little more than temporary sheds. Among them, only Ando's Garden of Fine Arts carried on the tradition of creating a complete universe in a single structure.

Moving among the columns, I could feel a refreshing breeze over the water and enjoy the glint of the sun on its surface. The irritation of having to negotiate miles of blazing asphalt pavement slipped quietly away. However one might judge the ceramic murals, there was much to be said just for the experience of walking here among the columns and over the water.

Ando's concern with restoring an awareness of nature comes close to being an obsession. Since any interest in nature had been completely abandoned in the rest of the fair pavilions, I felt increased respect for his skill in designing this one. At a fair held in the suburbs of the Osaka megalopolis, shouldn't far more emphasis have been placed on reawakening those responses to nature which have being lost in the midst of contemporary life? Indeed, should not all the architects have been more conscious of this theme?

Walking among the rows of columns, we are reminded that even in a contemporary city we need a modicum of nature. In this work Ando completely renounced architecture as a visual entity. Here, "architecture" ceased to possess so much as a façade; all that remained was plain, unadorned *space*. With even the walls omitted, what remained was no longer architecture as a physical object but architecture as experience. We found our sensibilities sufficiently enhanced to produce an awareness of the qualities of nature that still remain in the city but that usually go unnoticed. Architecture can still be a stage for this experience. In the same way, the arbors ("follies") situated around the exhibition grounds might be viewed as attempts to salvage the architecture-environment relationship from the old dichotomy of built structure versus natural environment.

Thus it was that, just about the time the bubble's collapse became immanent, a few architects, led by Tadao Ando, sensed a change and began to reflect a new era in their work.

# Osaka Prefectural Chikatsu-Asuka Historical Museum

The area of Minami Kawachi county, Osaka prefecture, near the border of Nara prefecture, is known as the site of hundreds of ancient burial mounds, including the burial place of Prince Shotoku (574-622), who first established the principles of civil government in Japan. The Chikatsu-Asuka Historical Museum was conceived to exhibit relics from those ancient times.

Chikatsu-Asuka Historical Museum, Minami Kawachi (Osaka): cascade stair in granite

Chikatsu-Asuka Historical Museum: head-on view of access ramp

Chikatsu-Asuka Historical Museum: stair and access ramp ▶

Chikatsu-Asuka Historical Museum: detail of stair

Taking a taxi from the nearby Kintetsu Railway, you travel some way through farmland and climb into the hills. Here you are greeted by an extensive granite-paved concrete slope that at a distance resembles a section of bleachers cut out of some immense sports stadium. Climbing up from one side into this "stadium," you embark upon a monumental stair that preempts your entire visual field, yet seemingly leads nowhere. In fact, the museum is half underground and the stepped slab doubles as a roof.

The stairway is rough cobbled in the white Mikage granite for which the Kansai region is famous. It measures several dozen yards along its variable width. But, surely enough, it leads nowhere, either at the top or at the foot: it is simply a huge stepped form in the midst of this history-laden landscape.

Sitting on the stairs, you gaze out at the valley and rounded hills. The roofs of farmhouses are scattered among the fields and orchards, a scene perhaps changed little in hundreds of years. It is easy to see why the ancients decided to settle in this broad and fertile-looking plain, with its mild climate and gentle terrain, then chose a monarch to found the state that launched Japanese history. Sitting there in the bright sunlight, thinking about the history of the plain stretching below, you begin to feel yourself merging into the landscape, caught up in the flow of history. Clearly, this staircase was positioned here as an historical vantage point.

Even given Ando's rigorous sense of proportion and discriminating choice of materials, a work of architecture is still diminutive in comparison with natural landscape. If the architect does not impart a sufficiently strong presence, the structure will prove insignificant. Human beings—more diminutive still than buildings—need some sort of physical backing or prop in order to confront such a powerful landscape and its history.

It was for that purpose that this vast stair was built. Ando's work faces nature squarely by virtue of its solidity. Held in the gentle embrace of that strength, we enjoy the stimulus of landscape and contemplate history. This stairway is the realization of a brand of modernism that imparts its own absolute beauty—of a kind expressed at one extreme in the Italian fascist architecture of Mussolini's era. A solid spatial anchor like this assures the firm backdrop against which an individual meets with nature, so to speak, on equal terms.

This building represents an interesting new approach to museum architecture, an endeavor not only to exhibit relics of the ancient past,

Chikatsu-Asuka Historical Museum: void over exhibition space

Chikatsu-Asuka Historical Museum: aperture

but also to give visitors an immediate sense of the surrounding terrain. After seeing the Chikatsu-Asuka Historical Museum, I could scarcely help thinking how much many other museums, located in the middle of a rich historical milieu, have lost. They are mere containers cut off from their surroundings and thus fail to help us gain a more genuine feel for history.

To reach the interior of the museum from the great stair you traverse a narrowly positioned ramp that slashes the cascade of stairs in the shadow of a high, poured-concrete wall. This is, in effect, a long, narrow passageway at the end of which are the mountains beyond. Entering this space after the bright sunlight of the stair, your sense of being pitted against the landscape gives way to the powerful presence of an internal architecture. From this transitional domain, you pass at last into the exhibition area.

The interior is a single immense exhibition hall arranged to be viewed initially while descending a ramp that cuts a wide arc at one end of the room. The exhibits are full of interest and easy to understand, but somehow seem to lack reality following the actual panorama outside. All the same, the composition and layout firmly supports the exhibit and amplifies the nature and quality of the artifacts.

After viewing the exhibit, I went outside again and walked from the very top to the bottom of the sea of steps. At the bottom, you find yourself at the borderline where man-made structure and nature vie with one another, and stretching out your hand, you could almost touch the trees. I left the museum thinking of ancient Japan, convinced that Ando's work had demonstrated something of the time-honored struggle between nature and human affairs.


# Rokko Housing

At the earliest stages of his Rokko Housing design, I heard Ando refer to the importance of "conception." This was at the beginning of the 1980s. By the importance or power of conception, Ando meant that, rather than the architect receiving a brief from the client that set the parameters of his work, the architect himself proposes a design that places the project in its most favorable social context. This approach Kenzo Tange had advocated, and it likewise reflects Ando's high-spirited idealism.

As has been noted earlier, the Rokko scheme was Ando's conception

Rokko Housing: model showing Phase I (at left) and Phase II

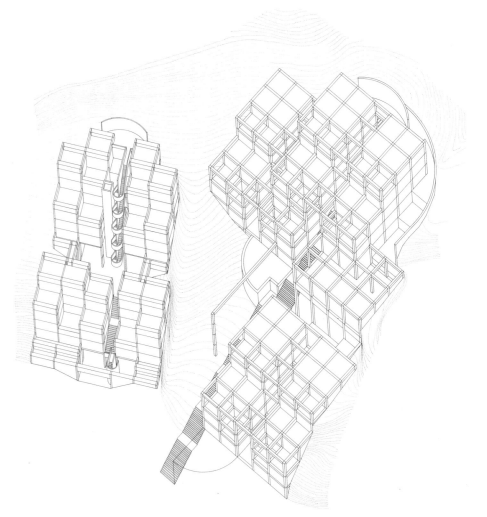

Rokko Housing: axonometric with Phase I (left) and Phase II

for transforming a cliff on the lower slopes of Mt. Rokko into an orderly community. Indeed, this project, which called for lopping off the side of a mountain to create tiered concrete housing, has turned out to be one of his most striking ongoing commissions. Several dozen dwellings were eventually erected on the slope, bringing into being a whole new community. The project expanded from this first cluster to a second, adjacent one. After the Kobe earthquake the owner of a neighboring site, Kobe Steel, asked Ando to design a third, and yet larger, cluster for their unmarried-employee housing.

Rokko Housing, by using controlled shapes, has totally changed the landscape in this area at the foot of Mt. Rokko. Yet it was not merely a matter of converting a natural landscape into an architectural unity, but rather of replacing various structures of utterly unrelated types and styles. It was thus an attempt to return a quality of serenity and order to the landscape. It is a difficult scheme to evaluate, however, owing to the characteristic disorder that still exists on the slopes beneath.

Nevertheless, we can again note here Ando's distinctive "landscape-creating" impulse. As I have stated, the first two phases of Rokko Housing wrought spaces with a strong centripetal power, their exterior stairways precisely calculated for effect. Of course, inasmuch as not only the spiraling stair, but also each living unit, affords an excellent view, nostalgic for me, of the city of Kobe and the sea beyond, this is also an exploratory work anticipating Ando's recent trend toward landscape creation. Ando stands firmly by the small box-like dwellings he so boldly experimented with from the beginning, with their ordered and articulate spaces, but in its totality Rokko Housing must be cited not merely for its gradually expanding scale but its significance in turning our attention back to nature.

Rokko Housing has been acclaimed on many points, and among these I would confirm the landscape vector. None of Ando's early works, including the first phase of Rokko Housing but with the sole exception of the Shitamachi Karaza theater, were meant primarily to "be seen." His interior space is always carefully articulated and his façades faithful to geometry, thus emblematic of the space inside. He observes this basic rule at Rokko, and here I find the three-phase development of his geometry elevated into a scheme that inscribes a specific hierarchy to space within nature.

Ando had stressed the project's conceptual nature, but what is most impressive to me is how he sticks to his first principles. The positions Ando takes on architecture, on its urban context, and on the environment are thoroughly consistent. His works are not intended to have an impact on the city or the environment in a self-conspicuous way. There may be shock value, paradoxically, in introducing startling primary colors or weird shapes to an already chaotic city, as some architects believe, but Ando does not hold with that trend. Throughout the twenty years of his career he has remained faithful to his initial approach, contriving simplified concrete forms, placing them carefully in the environment, and then biding his time to study their impact.

Once, when interviewing Togo Murano, an independent-minded modernist based in the Kansai region—and now considered to be among the masters—I was startled to hear him say, "No matter how garish the color of the tile used in the coffee shop next door to a building I am about to design, I always consider at least once the possibility of using the same type of tile." An architect of Murano's stature, I realized, knew the courtesy of giving attention to whatever may be built on an adjacent site. As for Ando, while he would almost certainly not use tile, he, too, is far from imposing his creations brashly on the surrounding environment. Quietly but with determination, he sets a work of his own aesthetic in place and then steps back to study the reaction. Indeed, he, too, is a master of architectural good manners, first cultivated in the urban milieu.

Ando has not abandoned this way of thinking about architecture even now in the 1990s, when his works are capable of having considerable impact on urban or natural landscape. Rokko Housing is a prime example of this unassuming approach. Smoothing the face of the cliff was labor intensive, but the rest—the building of these discreet, concrete boxes against it—transmitted the architect's intent to the surroundings without argument or fanfare. This is but a single piece of evidence showing that Ando possesses the necessary qualities for becoming a "landscape artist." We look forward to seeing what ultimate landscape the Rokko Housing scheme will create as the third-phase of the project comes into being after the disaster of the earthquake in Kobe.

# SPACE

▦

**W**hen we think of the nineteenth century and before, when palaces and mansions were decorated from floor to ceiling with ornate carvings and sensual murals depicting the human form, today's architecture comes across as somewhat brutal and cold. Since Ando's buildings of form-finished reinforced concrete take this contemporary style to its extreme, the layman may be rather at a loss to appreciate such works.

Our plain, undecorated architecture in the modernist style was once believed to correspond to the present age, as the Romanesque and Gothic did to medieval times, or Art Nouveau to the late nineteenth century. The basic principle of modernism, as articulated by the French architect Le Corbusier and other Europeans in the 1920s, is that buildings ought to make use of industrial materials. This, at any rate, has been the style considered appropriate to the twentieth century. The ornament and decor of previous architectural traditions, however beautiful and attractive, was held to be alien to an original aesthetic rooted in modern sensibilities.

The three principal materials of modernism are steel, glass, and concrete. Le Corbusier and other leaders of the modernist movement all used materials that could be mass-produced thanks to the technological advances of the industrial revolution; they poured their energies into creating a modern—by which they meant "rational" and functionalist— aesthetic. It soon became obvious that these materials did not yield a beauty understood and appreciated by the many. The reason people remain ill-disposed toward modern architecture is that these crude and unsophisticated materials were arbitrarily foisted upon them by architects, who simply insisted that we comprehend them *"because* they are modern."

In the complete absence of representational painting and decoration, the only architectural feature that might evoke beauty is *space*. None of the industrialized materials—steel, glass, or concrete—assert themselves forcefully in terms of either color or shape. The only option left to architects was to make use of these three in combination to carve out a "space" that, it was hoped, would resonate with the greatness of the universe. Box-like containers, neutral in tone, would have to offer an embodiment of beauty.

So *space* is everything, and the sense of proportion—depth, breadth, and height—that defines that space is nowadays the only factor that may be relied on for architectural expression. It is no easy task. The architect can no longer make use of any of the devices that pluck familiarly at the heartstrings of popular taste and sentiment. In fact, the challenge turned out to be so overwhelming that modernism was deadlocked by the 1970s and came to be superseded by postmodernism in the 1980s. The latter gave up on the sought-after modern aesthetic and revived older, more transparently representational styles of expression.

But Ando remained a staunch modernist, excluding all forms of representational expression. He has not joined the ranks of those who, in the belief that architecture is a communications device, grossly inject their buildings with metaphor and meaning. He has consistently and unfalteringly sought the abstract beauty of unapologetic modernism.

The architecture of Ando's predecessors in the Japanese wing of the modernist movement, apart from a few exceptions such as Kenzo Tange and Fumihiko Maki, is dead or defunct. Concrete walls have corroded and blackened, while renovations have been carried out to overcome the inconvenience of cramped interiors. The abstract beauty such modernist work was thought to embody has been all but obliterated. Yet Ando, who still defies—or challenges—us to discover beauty other than in the modern aesthetic, has not wavered from his original principles through a twenty-year career. His architectural ideal can be summed up by the concrete box.

When it comes to the degree of abstract perfection attainable in the verticals and horizontals of concrete, Ando's works have reached a plane far removed from that of his peers. So zealous is his quest that he spends hours on site, pouring concrete and adjusting forms himself. Ando's concrete is extremely solid and hard, which generally forestalls cracks from appearing on its even, gray surface. His first priority is construction, and his unremitting devotion and tireless energy on site is what makes it possible for him to achieve his designs in terms of their aesthetic of space.

Ando's approach to design resembles the ascetic's pursuit of truth. One might call it a religion. His studio attracts young people eager to share his arduous search, resolved to absorb from their mentor secrets not to be found in textbooks.

The spread of computer culture into the very fabric of daily life is rapidly eclipsing the mass-production–oriented technology of the industrial age upon which Le Corbusier's brand of modernism relied. Thus, modernism has increasingly ceased to speak for our times. Yet the task of perfecting this basic style of the twentieth century has not been achieved. Our contemporary world has been searching for someone capable of designing a space the way it should be done, and that search has led to Tadao Ando. While the engines of modernism remain stalled as the end of the century draws near, the world's attention is increasingly focused on this architect.

## Church of the Light

The name itself is intriguing and is sufficient to explain this building. Sure enough, it is a small concrete container. The texture of the exposed concrete exterior is typically Ando, though perhaps because it had to be built at very low cost, it is not quite as perfectly finished as many of his works. But the Church of the Light possesses a power that such minor flaws hardly diminish. It has the power of space and of light.

The church, which was built adjacent to the manse, I have declared to have the power of space, but it is essentially a box for preaching. The faithful come to sit, listen to the sermon, and pray, and nothing more. There are no lights in the ceiling, only a modest lamp at the front of the hall to illuminate the pulpit.

All other light is natural. Slits forming a large cross in the sanctuary wall behind the minister admit light from outside, creating an aura of sanctity and peace.

The light penetrates and passes up the steps of rough wooden pews one by one toward the back of the worship hall. It illuminates the concrete volume, etching itself into the darkness. The wooden floor is

Church of the Light: detail of pews and wooden flooring

◄ Church of the Light, Ibaraki (Osaka): sanctuary, looking toward chancel

painted pitch black in order to offset the illumination to optimal effect. Noiselessly this floor embraces the light as it advances toward the core of the church. All is plain and unobtrusive, enhancing the light's subtle dramatization of space.

The Church of the Light presents the culmination of modernism's ascetic space. There is no excess. There is no decorative effect. There is only space—and light. Still, the architecture fills us with quiet awe. We knew Ando's unerring sense of proportion even before this work. Now even more restrictions are placed upon the means of expression, but he has sharpened the spatial sense by reducing it to barest essentials, achieving thereby a quality of place far richer than heretofore.

As it happens, this church was constructed during 1988–89, just at the peak of the "bubble." This made it unexpectedly difficult for Ando and the local contractors to find skilled workers. But in the end each obstacle was overcome and the project brought to successful completion in a spirit of joyful determination.

Firm resolve is built into the walls of the Church of the Light. Like the chapels and cloisters of medieval Europe, whose powerful presence has been nurtured by accumulated memory over the last thousand years, this church is permeated with the genuine enthusiasm of all those involved. Pure-hearted devotion is, therefore, the starting point of the labor that will bring this church, too, to true completion a thousand years hence.

In a slightly unusual manner, pulpit and lectern are not raised high, but rather stand at the foot of the pews that are set on a gentle slope. Pastor Noboru Karukome has written that this arrangement symbolizes "Jesus Christ, who descended among men." Regarding Ando's heroic efforts to overcome financial strictures, he notes, "A church is not aloof from mundane affairs. It is directly linked to them. And yet, for all that, it is not a mundane place. The architect managed to resolve this very difficult dilemma."

These are much-needed words of encouragement for any architect. And Ando, in particular, has fought for what he achieved. From the Row House Sumiyoshi at the very start of his career, he has always coped with difficult constraints of some sort, and he has brought great satisfaction to his clients, and to society at large, by overcoming the odds. Knowing this, Pastor Karukome approached Ando to do his church, and Ando responded to the confidence placed in him by making the Church of the Light a kind of summation of his integrity and goals.

The eventual collapse of the overheated Japanese economy left peo-

Church of the Light: apse end and cross ▶

Church of the Light: view of cross from lectern

ple feeling bereft of all they had believed in. Even religion turned sour, as the followers of a misguided apocalyptic cult perpetrated one of the most shocking incidents in Japan's history at about this time, arousing intense debate over the relationship of reason to faith.

The Church of the Light rises above these minor blips of history. With its thoroughly modern space firmly earthbound, it prompts us to ask ourselves what truly enriches and fulfills human life. Indeed, one could say that this is just the role a church ought to play in modern society.

## Times

"Times" is built directly alongside the Takase River in the eastern part of Kyoto, in actuality a narrow canal dug in the seventeenth century, once plied by the low-draft *takasebune* boats that carried convicts away to exile, but today a shallow, cobble-paved stream. A modest but elegant commercial structure of shops and boutiques, with three above-grade floors and one at the level of the canal, "Times" has proved a landmark work. It awakened interest among the people of Kyoto in the qualities of urban space, forcing them to reconsider the assets their city could offer.

The name of the Takase canal has acquired a certain romance from its mention in familiar works of literature, yet until recently it was one of Kyoto's most neglected remaining waterways, its channel polluted and its banks lined with exhaust-billowing traffic. Taking note of the buildings up and down the canal in the neighborhood of "Times," one quickly sees how they turn their backs on it, snubbing its potential amenity with heaving air-conditioning condenser units, filthy exhaust ducts, and rusting drain pipes. Environments like this perpetuate the vicious circle of shunned ugliness in the city.

"Times" occupies an ideal commercial location, even in terms of busy downtown Kyoto, on the corner of the major Sanjo Avenue and the Takase River. Rejecting the sad precedent of its neighbors, Ando elected to face the building toward the canal. Airy corridors along the canalside were designed on each floor, where at the second and third levels visitors are able to lean on the railings and gaze up and down the waterway; at basement level, there is a kind of simulated landing where you can linger on a bench to enjoy the sight and sound of water flowing nearby.

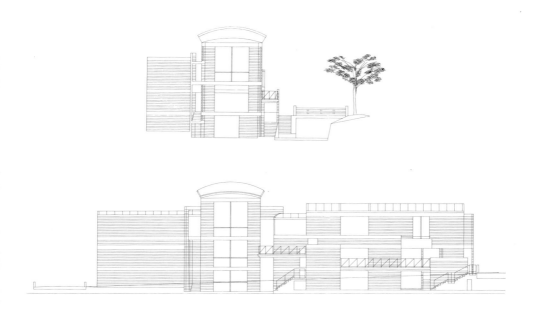

Times, Kyoto: lateral and riverfront elevations

Though purposely understated in architectural terms, the design did not fail to achieve its intended effects. Women coming to shop at the boutiques now pause on its terrace and balconies to look out over the canal, and their presence is soon noticed by people passing along busy Sanjo Avenue. Curiosity about "Times" went far to promote Ando's reputation among Kyotoites. The building also sparked a reevaluation of the Takase canal.

Rivers and canals were once important assets of most Japanese cities in terms of both infrastructure and townscape. Like the Seine in Paris—incidentally, Kyoto's sister city—or the Thames, waterways are an inextricable part of the story of older cities. Urban development since the early nineteenth century, however, has moved implacably forward through abuse and exploitation of rivers and other channels. In virtually all cities without proper drainage, rivers and creeks became filthy sewers, and no one seemed to care. Of Kyoto's rivers, the Kamo had been appreciated and looked after, but no such attentions were lavished on the Takase canal. A few minutes' walk from "Times" there is a boating wharf, but in the real life of the city it was despised as unworthy of notice.

Although the client demanded an efficiency-first structure for com-

Times: canal frontage (Takase River)

Times: waterfront promenade and Takase River

Times: view from Sanjo Avenue with promenade at lower left ▶

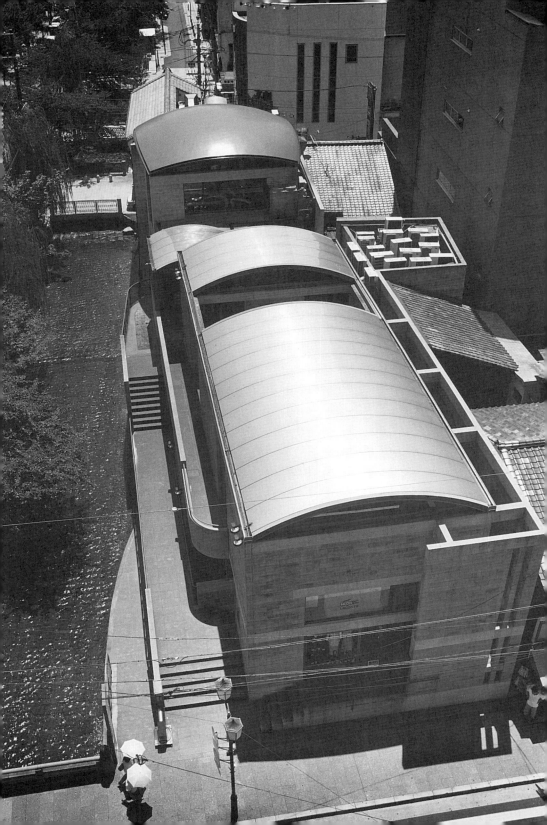

Times: from opposite bank

mercial use, Ando succeeded in arguing that "Times" should have open spaces facing the canal, thus holding out for amenity. "Times" and its architect are, therefore, to be praised for having offered a firm answer to the perennial question of what kind of architecture serves people.

Here again, what Ando realized in "Times" was not so much architectural *form*, but rather *space*. Many commercial buildings throughout Japan are designed, sometimes literally, like fairy-tale castles aimed at giving shape to a user's presumed visions of the ideal, but it is hard to tell whether this is actually a form of service or gratuitous condescension. What Ando sought to do at "Times" was to avoid this sort of image-centeredness by offering a simple "space" where people might naturally congregate.

With "Times," the architect's rebuilding of the canalside space that had long been forsaken and shunned won prompt popular support. Proceeding through the indirectly lit street-like spaces of "Times," the sense of release as one emerges onto the lower terrace or the balconies facing the river is impressive and dramatic. Here is all the drama of the city told by a small, commercial structure on a canal. No doubt its success gave Ando considerable satisfaction. It is easy to talk about the need to reappraise the value of waterways in urban areas, but architects are in a position to do more than talk; as Ando has shown, they can put the idea into practice. If more architects were thus ready to create works that truly contribute to the enhancement of the city, confidence in the architectural profession would doubtless be renewed. The success of the initial "Times" project led to the building of "Times II," also bordering the canal, and still more recently "Times III," both extensions of the original scheme. This has meant that for an entire block stretching south of Sanjo Avenue, buildings now enliven the canal.

Elsewhere, the Kamo River's image has long benefited from the tradition of the temporary restaurants (*yuka*) built out above the river's largely dry channel in summertime—a welcome attraction of the city's hot, humid summer. They survived because they fostered intimacy between the citizenry and their rivers as well as offering an ingenious form of relief from the sweltering heat. Today, thanks to Ando, a new interest has been taken in such treasured and practical traditions in other localities as well. The modest success of "Times" in reconstructing a relation between architecture and landscape—not as mere nostalgia, but as part of contemporary urban life—deserves high praise. This small commercial center must be counted as one of Ando's most outstanding achievements.

# Izutsu House

One does not learn the ways and manners of a city overnight. Like Tokyo, where you are entitled to boast of being part of the "Edokko" ethos only if you have lived there for at least three generations, every city fosters distinctive elements of lifestyle which newcomers strive to acquire if they wish to be accepted. And yet, as time goes by, these fundamentals are transformed, patterns of human activity change, and the lifestyles that once provided models begin to vanish. When this happens, various questions arise, such as what houses ought to look like.

For Ando, much of whose work is concerned with residential buildings in the history-rich Kansai area, the matter of how to respond to local tradition offers a constant challenge. In the Izutsu House (Townhouse at Kyujo Avenue) in the old commercial district of Osaka, we get a close look at Ando's way of responding.

The house is consistent with many previous small-scale dwellings in Ando's typical bare-concrete box-like style. Its three stories of form-finished concrete, on a site of roughly 720 square feet, rise a story or so higher than the buildings around it. Its beautifully finished concrete surfaces reveal little. The neighborhood has corners ablaze with the colorful advertising signs of bars and game parlors. The fact that the building does not dispute its entertainment-district surroundings is another policy to which Ando has remained faithful since the early phase of his career.

Inside, the building is characteristically unadorned: the contrast of exposed concrete with the grain of the plain wooden cabinetry is simple and cool. Ando had told me that the owner was an older woman who ran an *okonomiyaki* restaurant. He had also pointed out the urbane and sophisticated aesthetic (*iki*) of the people in the area, his remark reflecting a vivid admiration for the aesthetic sense of the ordinary people who have lived all their lives in the city.

Like Row House Sumiyoshi, this house imposes certain inconveniences on its inhabitants. To get from one floor to another, they must use an exterior stairway. This is one of the things you have to put up with, says Ando, in order to adapt such a small site for living, and besides, he declares, it is a good thing once in a while not to forget the feel of wind and rain. By prodding his clients to "enjoy" such inconveniences, Ando asks them to further temper their urbanity.

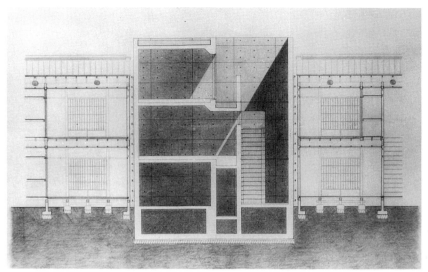

Izutsu House, Osaka: with *tsuboniwa* at center

Izutsu House: detail of stair

In this house, the concrete walls immediately abut the adjacent dwelling. Ascending the stairs to the second and third floors, one notices a space approximately two yards square at the very back, included within the walls but open clear to the top of the building. This roofless space exposed to the elements is paved with pitch black semi-glazed pantiles (*gensho-seki*). I immediately recognized it as a minimalist version of the classic *tsuboniwa* garden.

As a student, I had often visited townhouses in Kyoto, with their long, narrow floor plans in what has been dubbed an "eel-trap" design. Along one side of the ground floor of these houses is an earthen-floored area from which one enters the house and where the kitchen is also located. And no matter how small the house, there is invariably a one-*tsubo*-square (the space of two tatami or about four square yards) garden adjacent to the formal sitting room.

As the name implies, a tsuboniwa is a garden that may be as small as one tsubo planted with a few modest ornamental shrubs and seasonal flowers and perhaps containing a small stone lantern. Even Kansai-ites, known for their shrewdness and for having lived in high-density environments since ancient times, and who might be expected to quickly dispense with such "extraneous" space, invariably find a place to tuck in a tsuboniwa.

These diminutive gardens were devices by which people managed to cling to nature, otherwise so easily forgotten amid the crowding and bustle of the city. By just opening the *shoji* partitions, they could feel the breezes of the season and smell the fragrance of rain-drenched plants and flowers. What good was life, it was thought, without having a spot of nature at arm's reach. And thus the tsuboniwa became an indispensable, if at first glance seemingly "wasted," component of every residence, a device of traditional acumen and wisdom that sustained human sanity within the city.

The Izutsu House tsuboniwa is, of course, based on the same principle as the traditional version. When rain falls, the black ceramic paving blocks turn from dusty gray to a dark, lacquer-like sheen. In this modern dwelling, the sheer surrounding walls rise up to the third floor, making the tsuboniwa look from above rather like the bottom of a well, an effect dramatized by rain. When the wind swirls through this well-like space, one feels to an ever greater degree the palpable presence of nature within the city.

Structures that merely imitate tradition, by casting the classic wooden forms of temple or shrine architecture in concrete, can hardly be said to transmit history in any true sense. What Ando's houses teach us is that it is more important to be faithful to the *spirit* of tradition, in which it is space (rather than form) that plays the significant role. In the Izutsu House, we note this in the paradoxical emptiness (*ku*) that is symbolic of the fullness of its tsuboniwa.

Through such spatial devices, contemporary city dwellers are able to sustain spiritual links with their predecessors of the Kyoto townhouse prototype and thus continue to live comfortably in high-density environments. Ando's Izutsu House affords its inhabitants that opportunity.

# Koshino House

In the comfortable Hanshin suburb of Ashiya is a lush green district called Okuike, an upscale residential area in the foothills of Mt. Rokko where houses are, by Japanese standards, more like resort homes in both style and scale. The house Ando built here for fashion designer Hiroko Koshino is perhaps the finest of his early-period works.

The green of the surroundings sets off the crisp, clean lines of grayish concrete. Ando's strict geometry deployed in the midst of a natural landscape presents graceful forms quite different from his works situated in more densely crowded areas of the city below. The site slopes steeply, with the streetside entrance at the highest point, and the body of the house tucked snugly into the slope.

The first view of the house from the street is striking. Beyond the entrance, which Ando has marked with a semi-circular concrete apron surrounded by green lawn, the flat roof of a rectangular monolithic volume is visible. In the bright sunlight, the concrete is dazzling yet solemn. No work reveals an architect's skill so clearly as a detached abstract structure such as this house, because there is no element that takes away from the full appreciation of its geometry.

Ando's building is situated squarely on the site. The concrete volumes—so incongruous that one might think for a moment of alien shapes dropped from outer space—are of quite otherworldly beauty with their precise horizontals, clean 90-degree corners, and utterly parallel roof planes.

If you visit the West Coast of the United States, you come across a number of modern-style dwellings designed by well-known architects. They pursue the same sort of modernist geometry as Ando in the Koshino

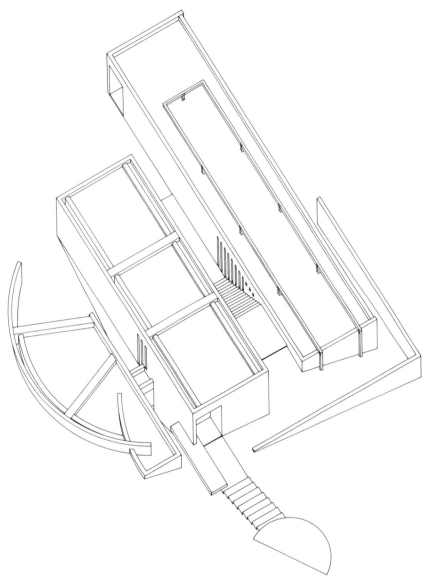

Koshino House, Okuike (Ashiya) near Kobe: axonometric

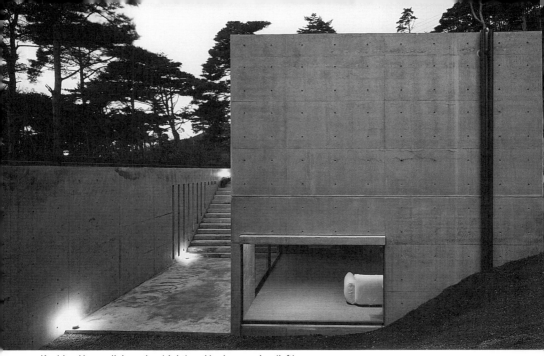

Koshino House, living wing (right) and bedroom wing (left)

Koshino House: living room interior

Koshino House: detail of living-room wall

House, though frequently on a scale many times greater. In the wide-open Western spaces, these structures rise up in all their modernist glory, in ideal settings, carefree and with practically no restrictions or limits.

Although perhaps inferior in physical scale to such American examples, the Koshino House stands out even in such distinguished company because of Ando's unrivalled devotion to his material, maintained since the start of his career. Because of Ando's determination to coax from concrete a geometry such as the world had never seen, he led the work at the site, exhorting his whole staff to the task, and brought a masterpiece into being.

Inside, Ando skillfully harnessed the resources of natural light, enlivening his space with light and shadow. Natural light, ingeniously let in through adroitly situated slits in ceiling and walls, disperses the darkness and creates a pleasantly habitable space.

We had seen this manipulation of light in Ando's earlier small houses, but perhaps because of the larger scale of this dwelling, the play of light and shadow he orchestrates is effective throughout, most famously in the central living space, resulting in an easy spaciousness that is qualitatively different from what he had achieved in smaller works.

Ando used virtually no light fixtures in the Koshino House. The subsidiary living areas, which are children's rooms lining the lower-level hallway, are illuminated chiefly by simple wall fixtures. This was deliberate, for Ando was determined to allow only pure space dependent on the simplest materials, concrete, and the light of day.

Houses that have become classics in the history of modernism, like Mies's diminutive Farnsworth House and Philip Johnson's Glass House in New Canaan, demonstrate through the articulation of geometry in lush landscapes that the architect's universe can rival that of nature. Ando's Koshino House, too, possesses something of this quality. Initially I was curious, and not a little concerned, since Ando had first established his architectural ground on compact urban terrain in response to cramped building sites and numerous other difficulties. What would he do, I wondered, given a spacious, open arena in which to perform? The Koshino House proved at once that we had only witnessed the tip of Ando's creative iceberg.

Although he is today widely engaged with projects for public building on a much grander scale than the Koshino House, the only other dwelling Ando has designed so far on a scale equal to what is common in other parts of the world is the spacious Kidosaki residence in Tokyo.

Simply put, the opportunity seldom presents itself. No doubt I am not alone in hoping that Tadao Ando will soon be able to use his recently evolved techniques of "landscape-creating" architecture in the space of further residential experiments.

Koshino House: exterior of bedroom wing

# Row House Sumiyoshi

The unfamiliar coinage *hikari-niwa* (here translated as "light court") became current among Japanese architects only after Ando's Row House Sumiyoshi was constructed in Osaka in 1976. A tiny concrete volume built to replace the middle unit of a group of three wooden row houses and occupying only 540 square feet, this dwelling brought Ando instant fame.

The *nagaya* row house is an established form of economy duplex, or triplex, housing that is widespread in urban districts of the Kansai area. The client requested the rebuilding of the central unit as a two-story, poured-in-place concrete box. The original dwelling was of the typical long-narrow "eel-trap" shape, and at the heart of that slender typology Ando installed his "light court." Enclosed on both sides by walls and situated at its center, the light court divides the house into a central open space enclosed by segments in front and behind. The latter are separated at ground level by the courtyard and joined on the second floor by a concrete bridge.

While, as the term implies, sunshine pours into the light court in good weather, in bad the outdoor space is inevitably swept by wind and rain. Since the dwelling has a footprint of only 30 *tsubo*, one might think such a design rather wasteful of prime space. But, of course, Ando had his reasons. He likes to argue that the longer we of the modern age dwell in cities, the more seriously our sensitivity to the fluctuations of the seasons is eroded. To dwell is also to live, so even in a house of minimal size, there is need for inhabitants to reawaken their consciousness of nature by, for example, having to put up an umbrella when going from one part of the house to the other in the rain.

People were excited and inspired by this kind of architecture. From the gloom that beset modern architecture emerged Ando, who had entered the profession without training by way of the usual academic route. His ideas on the nature of the city offered a completely new perspective—an "ant's eye" view, so to speak—that was warmly welcomed.

Row House Sumiyoshi is impressive enough to convince us that Ando was right. The concrete, to which the architect had paid close attention, personally leading the work of settling it in the forms with a bamboo pole, is solid, its purity enhanced by his rigorous sense of proportions. As a result, connoisseurs of Ando's work claim that what is ostensibly just another concrete volume possesses an awe-inspiring

◀ Koshino House: corridor detail

**153**

Holographic sketch of existing row houses (Tadao Ando)

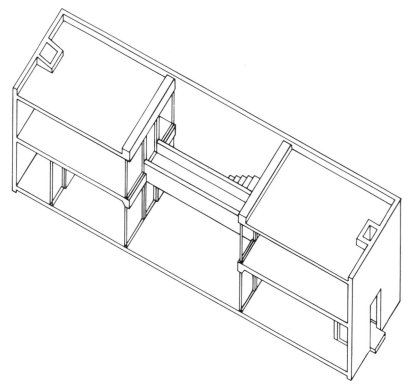

Row House Sumiyoshi, Osaka: axonometric

Row House Sumiyoshi: detail of light court

quality not to be found in any other example of form-finished concrete. I myself cannot tell whether Ando's architecture really possesses this awesomeness, of which such persons so blithely speak. Still, I am convinced that there is a certain aura akin to obsession that clings to Ando's work in reinforced concrete, something that cannot be calculated by tangible measure.

Still Ando could scarcely have won the accolades of critics if all he had to offer was his "light court." In a noted essay on the Yasuda Insurance Tower in Tokyo's new West Shinjuku business district, the well-known architectural historian and critic Teiji Itoh favorably contrasted Ando's Sumiyoshi Row House with recent high-rise architecture. What attracted Itoh, a scholar of seasoned judgment and sensibilities, to this simple concrete dwelling was, I believe, the sure-handed way in which space was backed by the integrity of materials.

It is not an easy task to appraise space, which is essentially void, and still be persuasive. Yet Ando's architecture profers such attractive spaces that one is reluctant *not* to tackle the subject. We can see why ordinary people in the mid-1970s were revolted by the methods of a devalued modernism with its ready-to-assemble frames ordered from factory catalogues. To models of efficiency-first modernism, such as the Yasuda Insurance block cited by Itoh, which render the city bland and barren, Ando's light court offered an antithesis, marked by the illogical necessity of an umbrella to negotiate a tiny dwelling.

People came to realize that the true measure of a timeless way of building was not scale, not cost, nor degree of elaboration: what was required was a spiritual element. This was the essence of what Ando was trying to accomplish, its expression nothing more or less than the spaces he characteristically designed. The Japanese architectural world began to accord Ando, then a young Osaka-based architect in his mid-thirties, a grudging esteem.

The backlash against modernism was propelled further by the bubble economy, resulting in a return to a pre-abstract vocabulary and a nostalgia for history. But like a boxer with his eye firmly trained on a punching bag, Ando paid scant attention to these things; instead, he continued to mold "space." Whatever distortions the "bubble" mentality produced in the Japanese building and construction world, it did not modify Ando's position in the least.

# HISTORY

⠿

For a contemporary architect in pur-
suit of originality, history can be a burden. If he wants to create something
completely new and fundamentally revolutionize people's perceptions
of space, history stands in the way. Every new undertaking must inevitably do battle with convention and custom, and is at first castigated
as outlandish and looked upon with suspicion and distrust.

It was once assumed that twentieth-century architects would pursue
their art without concern for history, that they would be forever in the
vanguard of their time. Students were told over and over that the basic
rule of creative originality amounted to casting off the fetters of history
and tradition. Ando, too, was raised in this ethos, and he thrived on it
and was recognized.

Tadao Ando's debut as an architect twenty years ago happened to
coincide with the period when the profession was gripped by uncon-
cealable deadlock. History had reasserted itself. People began to resist,
and then reject, unsubstantial modernist structures made of industrialized materials, and architects found themselves at a loss to defend the
"style" they had identified with their century.

The strategic retreat to the proposition that architecture is only an
extension of history ushered in postmodernism. Architects resorted, for
lack of a better alternative, to reincorporating in contemporary designs
the kinds of spaces that ordinary people thought of as enriching and
attractive. In the wake of this revived historicism, cityscapes the world
over began to sprout skyscrapers with spires and conical roofs. Arata
Isozaki wryly described the new trend as "postmodern Déco," drawing

a comparison with the Art-Déco vogue that spawned 1920s and 1930s Manhattan.

But Tadao Ando paid no attention to the postmodern fashion. Never doubting that truth lay in the aesthetic of modernism, he went on building his exquisitely crafted concrete boxes. His goal was to bring to fulfillment several thousand years of architectural history leading up to the end of the present century.

At the same time, Ando humbly acknowledged that even modernism draws sustenance from history. History is accumulation, and the aesthetic of bare essentials he seeks in the modernist style derives from the ancient science of proportions originated by the Greeks and Romans. He accepts this coexistence with older architecture and, when a brief calls for retaining a sense of history in the urban context, he does so without grandstanding and with due respect.

The greatest architects of the modernist era produced superlative work even when making use of past styles. Kenzo Tange's recent Tokyo City Hall complex and his adjacent Shinjuku Park Tower building demonstrate an admirable skill at reviving history in the modern age, which perhaps can only be hoped for from such a master.

And what about Ando? In Fabrica, in part a project to restore a seventeenth-century Italian villa, he was attentive to the context of the surrounding countryside, blending history and contemporaneity. In his still more recent Oyamazaki Museum, which also included the renovation of an older Western-style structure, he forged an ingenious link with Japan's architectural heritage.

In the Honpukuji Water Temple on Awaji Island, with its lotus-pond roof and below-grade structure quite unlike any temple ever built, Ando achieved an awe-inspiring contemporary monument to the legacy of Buddhism. There was also the Shitamachi Karaza theater, with its unique silhouette bringing to mind medieval Japanese architecture—a crystallization of contemporary dramatic art set on one of the city's least-favored sites.

Ando was widely criticized for his scheme to construct an egg-shaped auditorium within the existing structure of the Nakanoshima Public Assembly Hall, for which a competition had been sponsored as part of a historical district proposal for Nakanoshima, Osaka. That plan, however, was deferred and has since been realized in the Inamori Hall at Kagoshima University.

These were all projects professing a multi-dimensional interpretation of history one might never have expected of an architect whose ultimate goal is to create beauty in bare concrete. These works were not the progeny of any postmodern-Déco fashion; each displays only the exquisite, carefully honed forms unique to Ando's architecture. Looking back over his career, we can see that for Ando the encounter with a specific architectural artifact has often posed an important artistic challenge.

So-called postmodern Déco ended up a flash in the pan; it lost its freshness almost as soon as it became popular mannerism. Media society is always a hotbed of imitation. It not only assimilated postmodern Déco but has likewise focused on Ando's own exposed-concrete style. Still, Ando has succeeded in showing, through a series of works in which the contemporary overlays or undergirds the historical, that he has nothing to do with mere pastiche. His capacity to incorporate other narratives into the adventure of modernism must now be seen as part of the fabulous secret of his concrete boxes.

## Benetton's Fabrica

What attitude should a Japanese architect take toward the long history of European architecture? When Ando was commissioned to design Fabrica, he found himself in a situation where he was unable to proceed without addressing this dilemma.

Luciano Benetton, the client, hoped, above all, that Ando would address coexistence of the historical and the contemporary. To commission an architect like Ando from either the United States or Japan to perform this task must be viewed as without precedent, and no doubt Ando himself was bewildered. After all, the hallmark of twentieth-century architecture is an orientation toward creative, original work; the question of coexistence with history barely enters in.

Benetton assigned Ando the task of making over a seventeenth-century villa of the Italian gentry into a school for young and talented artists from around the globe. While initially seeking a straightforward job of preservation, he knowingly chose an architect unlikely to stop at that. After hours of discussion between architect and client and the elapse of quite a bit of time, the sparring over ideas was settled in the design we see today. An artificial pond was made on the site, crossed by a bridge. Along this bridge extends a line of columns in unmistakably Ando-trademark exposed concrete. This assemblage of columns is like a hammer driven into the historical landscape with the full force of

Fabrica, Treviso: restoration (seventeenth century)

Ando's conviction, but these are his only forms visible from the exterior. He respected history by sinking the new lecture hall and library below grade behind the villa.

At the construction site, one's first impression was this respect for Italian architectural custom: creativity and innovation were exercised only after history was given its due. Inside the restored villa one discovers sophisticated new plasterwork and the gentle texture of wood, creating spaces such as we have never before seen in a work by Ando. The concrete forms identifiable as Ando's are all submerged. Gazing across the school's grounds, you do not miss the stern geometry by which we instantly recognize Ando's presence; instead you feel only a comforting sense of space that induces spontaneous relaxation.

You might think such a design signals the defeat of Ando's marvelously idiosyncratic creativity, but I would disagree. Ando has responded conscientiously to the program of the client. He has effectively changed his own tune out of deference to Italian climate and culture, and I believe this represents a considerable shift.

If all building in the twentieth century had taken this approach, architecture today would meet with less suspicion and resentment. Instead, contemporary architects, in their presumption to reshape the world on the strength of the experience of their own century alone,

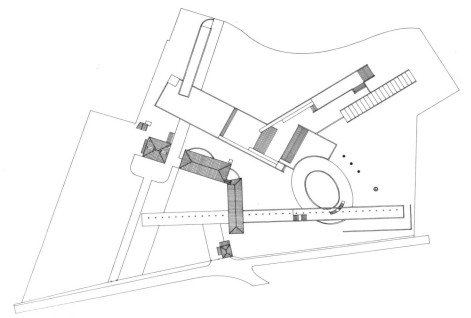

Fabrica: site plan

insist on designs and techniques that deliberately ignore the norms and values passed down through the ages. Some, who fail to appreciate his vocabulary, may regard Ando as such an architect.

Though Ando is believed to have maintained a consistent and pure modernism in his works, he has not ignored the historical landscape, as we can see from works like Rose Garden, with its brick-tile veneer, designed to take its place among the Western-style edifices of Kobe's historic Kitano district. This is one of the more outstanding of his early works; it proved that he could offer an original response while respecting the etiquette of tradition. This flexibility is one of the traits distinguishing Ando as an architect. It is what enabled him, once in contact with the Italian architectural milieu, to accommodate Benetton's wishes in preserving and restoring the old villa.

In a given environment, whether to remain uncompromising or to accommodate is often the decisive question for those working in the context of existing cities, as do most architects today. What separates the everyday from the extraordinary is the imaginative solution produced, even if it opts to compromise. Ando's decision to undertake the Fabrica project—his largest overseas project theretofore—on a theme combining history with contemporary architectural elements, only reflects his increased stature.

Fabrica: restoration and colonnade

There are many kinds of masterpieces. Truly significant works include not only those that challenge convention and demolish stereotypes but those that similarly seek to achieve a higher purpose, through restraint and tact. Clearly, Fabrica is a work belonging to this latter genre. Given the quiet rural setting, a policy of restraint was the most appropriate. The work, which has earned praise in Italy, also contains an important message for us as Japanese, with our scrap-and-build culture and all too often cavalier attitude toward history and the existing environment.

## Oyamazaki Museum

In the heady days of Japan's rapid economic growth, the question was often asked when history ends and the contemporary age begins. Any event predating the mid-nineteenth century, when modernization and industrialization began, was clearly history, but consensus seemed to waver regarding the latter part of the nineteenth century and became even more shaky toward the early decades of our own century or events on either side of World War II. Up until that time, the role of the Kansai area in the Japanese economy had been far greater than today. The elegant, ornate Western-style mansions built with the wealth that accumulated in the old cities of Kyoto and Osaka, as well as in the port of Kobe, should have constituted a substantial historical legacy, but most of those buildings were never given their due, partly since they were not considered as belonging to Japanese "history." Over the years many have vanished from sight and memory.

The Oyamazaki villa, residence of the Kansai businessman Shotaro Kaga, very nearly met this fate. Fortunately, Asahi Breweries, to whom ownership of the estate had fallen, and the Kyoto prefectural government determined to preserve and restore the house and outbuildings. In the spring of 1996 these were opened to the public as the Oyamazaki Museum.

I admit I was surprised to hear that Tadao Ando had been chosen to plan the museum. He designed a new art gallery, nicknamed the "underground treasure chest," but Ando seems even prouder of his restoration of the old Kaga country house at Oyamazaki. Ando was fascinated by the effort and enthusiasm Kaga had poured into this house. It was built in the characteristic half-timber manner—with exposed beams and white-washed walls—that Kaga first saw when he went to England as a student. Designed and built to Kaga's own taste by the Obayashi Construction Company, the house remains a luxurious and grand country house in the Western style.

Ando is convinced that Kaga's architectural dreams were most lavishly indulged in the large second floor terrace: "Oyamazaki commands a full view of the spot where the Katsura, Uji, and Kizu rivers converge; and the terrace is so large you never tire of the view." Indeed, the terrace is almost entirely covered by the sweep of the gable roof and is more spacious than the adjacent enclosure. We recognize immediately that the aim of the building was to take advantage of the spectacular view from this part of the site.

Such enthusiasm, says Ando, is the essence of good building. "The uprights are all far larger than needed. The spacious dimension of the terrace, the uncommonly sturdy beams—you may think these odd—but to me all this is proof of the owner's excitement over the building and the passion that made it genuine architecture. That is what I want people to see when they come here."

A plan was drawn up for preservation of the old villa, improvement of the surrounding gardens, and construction of a new wing. The "underground treasure chest" was designed by Ando as a small gallery half-submerged below grade, round with a skylight at its center to bring in natural light. The works housed here include a few paintings, among

Oyamazaki Museum, Kyoto: model of restoration and submerged gallery

Oyamazaki Museum: aerial view

which is a Monet, and a single sculpture. The gallery is certainly extravagant for such a modest display.

Ando committed himself to restoring Kaga's villa insofar as possible to its original state. Where later renovations had been made, he consulted the original drawings and undertook to restore with new materials, taking care to match colors and textures. I would venture to say, on Ando's behalf, that it takes courage for a contemporary architect to take on such a job. After all, the raison d'être for an architect of our times is original creation in accord with current values, so acknowledging even the recent past may seem out of the question. Nothing was more abhorrent, according to the prevailing view in Japan, than restoring part of a building with new materials deliberately made to look old. Scientific restoration of an ancient building using authentic materials would, of course, be another matter.

In any case, Ando declares that he experienced no hesitation or qualms in bringing back to life the spirit of Shotaro Kaga and passing it

Oyamazaki Museum: view of garden

Oyamazaki Museum: detail of new construction

on for future generations, whatever the means. I could not agree more. Architecture signifies, above all, three-dimensional space. What makes possible its existence over time is the "spirit" of that space, not the materials in which it is realized. This spirit is what distinguishes the architecture of Japan's great Shinto shrines, despite the fact that they have been rebuilt countless times, as well as the cathedrals of Europe that were rebuilt from the ashes of war using the means best suited to their preservation from century to century.

Perhaps because our tradition of architecture is largely one of wood—a material of limited durability—Japanese tend to be fussy about original materials. Preoccupied with reverence for structures that have miraculously survived the ravages of history, our view may have become rather narrow. And since Japan actually possesses the world's oldest wooden buildings, our judgment of works that postdate the beginning of the modern era may be rather harsh.

Those who know Ando and his architecture may be bemused to see that his revival of the past at Oyamazaki Museum accords greater respect to history than to contemporary design. But Ando seems to have mellowed by the time he undertook this project. He had become an architect at once less self-assertive and more deeply concerned about history.

What he had learned in the course of building Benetton's Fabrica was certainly instrumental in producing this change. He had also discovered the truth that the spiritual dimension of architecture is essentially an outcome of the enthusiasm of the person behind the work. This insight no doubt inspired him to take up the challenge of the Oyamazaki restoration.

## The Honpukuji Water Temple

The most important issue in architecture should always be the "spirit" of space. Architecture that is truly part of history should not merely express nostalgia for the past; it should link history to the present. This is not difficult to accomplish if it involves only superficial aspects of form. But the exercise can easily end up a kind of cultural taxidermy, which does nothing to pass on an intrinsic—that is, living—spirit. Nor is architecture the only endeavor in which the transmission of spirit between past and present gives rise to difficulties.

At first glance, Ando's Honpukuji temple hardly seems to emulate the past in terms of forms. It is a world of abstraction: the main volume a buried cylinder, the lotus-pond roof a circle, the entrance an arced wall. And yet we should not imagine this temple, with its cemetery containing the graves of generations past, to be cut off from history.

Indeed, as noted in the first part of the book, Ando at Awaji did not in the least betray the expectations of parishioners. As soon as you enter the main sanctuary of his concrete structure, you find yourself

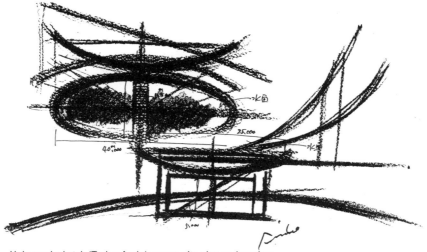

Holograph sketch (Tadao Ando): composite plan and section

immersed in history. The apertures, as will be recalled, are fitted with lattices painted scarlet, allowing natural light to filter through with dramatic effect. Orange rays that appear to shine directly out of the Buddhist Western Paradise thus penetrate every corner of Ando's hall at Honpukuji. In a space without artificial illumination, natural light must play the role of protagonist, and by causing that light to dye the room red, so to speak, Ando has given expression to the existence of Amida's Western Paradise.

The notion that plain exposed concrete is similar to the undecorated beauty of natural wood was a typical constructional analogy modernists evolved in their attempt to relate traditional Japanese architecture and modern rationalism. But for those outside the architectural profession, such ideas were difficult to grasp. Ando's architecture helps us to understand this modern aesthetic. As you witness the scene at Honpukuji temple, with its hall illuminated by a shower of light from behind the sacred image of Amida, you are almost involuntarily persuaded that the bare concrete is a canvas of infinite potential, endowed with a quality akin to natural wood.

Here, "form" is not at issue. The goal is obtained through a dramatic effect of light in a way that goes back to Chogen's temple Jodoji, built in the early Kamakura period (1192-1333). This design is not only a direct evocation of Chogen's technique but also the expression of conventions recalling what Japanese people believe temple architecture

Honpukuji Water Temple, Awaji Island: view of lotus pond

should be. How to embody such traditions in a contemporary building must be left to the judgment of the architect. Some might choose to reflect them in "form." But, here at Honpukuji, Ando succeeded in transmitting a legacy not through form but simply by embracing light.

In this respect, I believe, Ando has grasped *spirit*—the essence of architecture, the soul of the architect, and an abstract expression of modernism. The Honpukuji Water Temple came into being as a contemporary religious structure at the meeting point of these three considerations.

Descending the stairway that slices into the pond with its blossoming lotus, one is plunged into the blessed realm of spirit. In this completely original composition, Ando accomplishes much more than merely passing on the legacy of tradition.

In the 1960s, several prominent architects tried their hand at temple architecture in concrete. However, save for the Zenshoji Main Hall designed by Seiichi Shirai and the Isshinji Temple designed by its own resident priest, Yasuyuki Takaguchi, none evoked genuine spirit. In time, such projects ceased to pique the interest of architects and were all but forgotten until Ando's Honpukuji.

Ando once more achieved spirituality in his Church of the Light at Ibaraki (Osaka) for the United Church of Christ in Japan. Although the two buildings serve different religions, both epitomize the modernist conviction that "an aesthetic of poverty expresses the greatest richness." Both create realms of the spirit admirably transcending East and West.

From a different perspective, Honpukuji might be seen as the antithesis of the wave of postmodern Déco that has swept architecture since the latter half of the 1980s. If the return to older representational styles of architecture that flourished in the recent spate of waterfront projects is emblematic of materialist concerns at the end of this century, what Ando sought in his design for Honpukuji is totally opposite.

This work lay almost at the epicenter of the mammoth tremor that caused so much destruction in January 1995, now known as the Great Hanshin Earthquake. It is a cruel irony that disaster should visit a place like Awaji, a world away from the extravagances of conspicuous consumption and the excesses of the bubble economy. Mercifully undamaged, Honpukuji became a refuge for the surrounding communities as they strove to rebuild and to resume normalcy.

◀ Honpukuji Water Temple, Main Hall: detail of lattice

Shitamachi Karaza, Asakusa (Tokyo): construction detail beneath dome

# Shitamachi Karaza

Every city has traditions, both relating to the whole and to each of its neighborhoods. In Tokyo, too, something remains of the characteristic local flavor of various sub-centers, despite the homogenization that has rendered history virtually invisible in much of the megalopolis.

Locating the Shitamachi Karaza on the banks of the Sumida River in Asakusa was appropriate because the district was once a center of popular theater. In the 1920s and 1930s, this area of Tokyo had seen a number of experimental avant-garde theaters. Juro Kara ambitiously attempted to revive the Asakusa/Shitamachi area as a focus for the small-theater movement by forming a new theatrical group and building a mobile theater. By his participation, Ando embarked on new territory for his architecture.

A decade has passed since then, and today, as we contemplate the collapse of the bubble economy and subsequent recession, we can see that the Shitamachi Karaza was an extravagant and provocative project that would never gain support today.

Perhaps only now, in retrospect, do we realize how much this project was inspired by Ando's ideas about Japanese-style architecture. It is astonishing that he could have fashioned that mobile theater, with its conical roof and a half-moon-bridge entrance, out of scaffolding pipe and concrete formwork. When the theater opened, those materials were so beautifully integrated into the Japanese-style structure that one hardly noticed. The vast majority of the audience was unaware that the theater where they sat had been built of rough engineering elements.

Using such equipment for a finished structure, however temporary, is of course a completely modernist idea, far removed from any Japanese tradition. Ando's virtuosity is plain in the way he forged a link between the two.

True Japanese-style architecture was rarely built of carefully selected, high-quality materials, but belonged instead to a sophisticated spiritual tradition, in which, following the tea masters of old, secondhand and odd-shaped timbers were selected for their roughness, patina, and distinctive character. If the archetypes of the *wabi/sabi* tea room relied on salvaged timber, irregular beams, and time-worn posts, the "*new* Japanese style," Ando seemed to suggest, could be built with the steel pipe and concrete formwork one can find heaped up in any construction storage yard. Through this scheme Ando asserted that the unseen beauty

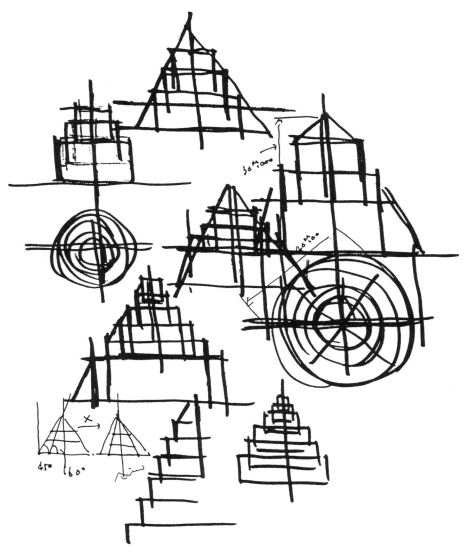

Holograph sketch (Tadao Ando) depicting variants of Shitamachi Karaza

of such materials could provide a genuine Japanese style for the contemporary age. His approach remained true to the aims of modernism: to reveal beauty by eliminating decoration and allowing materials natural expression through the medium of architecture itself.

Japanese architecture is based on a post-and-beam module, making it fundamentally different from the earliest Western architecture, built of brick or masonry. Westerners like Frank Lloyd Wright and Le Corbusier developed a strong interest in traditional Japanese building, partly because twentieth-century structural systems were essentially of the nonload-bearing, post-and-beam type.

One of the reasons that Ando may have embarked on the Shitamachi Karaza adventure was his desire to respond to sentiment from overseas that contemporary Japanese architects ought to address themes derived from their own tradition. This was his answer in the modern age to the principles behind seventeenth-century *sukiya* architecture, like that of the Katsura Imperial Villa. Following the Karaza project, he went on to design a temporary structure for Bishin Jumonji, a prominent photographer; it was similarly based on Ando's exploration of Japanese style in the late-1980s.

It is probably no accident that this interlude in Ando's career coincided with the height of the bubble economy. He showed not the slightest interest in compromising his aesthetic in the lucrative developer projects that were seducing most architects, but instead poured his efforts into Japanese-style works made with scaffolding pipe and rough planks. Instinctively aware of the pitfalls, he staunchly resisted the lure of big money to be made from lending one's name as "design supervisor" for distant, large-scale projects. Instead, he occupied himself with a mobile theater, in which the glittering guests invited for the opening night were so cold they resorted to wrapping newspaper around their legs.

The phantom-like sight of the Shitamachi Karaza silhouetted for a while on the banks of the Sumida in Asakusa remains memorable. With its black siding and red roof ensconced on the riverbank, the theater was eerily exotic. A theater by nature is another world created within this one, and the lines of theatergoers streaming up and over the Karaza's half-moon bridge recalled the multitudes traveling from this world to the next.

In our post-bubble times, architecture that creates a sensation in the city has become somewhat rare. The Shitamachi Karaza now seems a shining moment in the architectural history of Tokyo. Crystallizing ideas and hopes—as well as certain disagreements among its creators— and overcoming at last all the odds and difficulties, this theater gave

Queue at Shitamachi Karaza

real form to their vision. Many of us will long remember this anti-bubble Japanese-style work, which showed us what one architect's committed vision could achieve, if only briefly.

## Inamori Hall, Kagoshima University

When Ando first presented a proposal for the restoration of Osaka's Nakanoshima Public Assembly Hall, I must confess I was taken aback. It was a bold—no, unbelievable—plan to preserve the exterior of the hall, while inserting within it a vast egg-shaped capsule.

The original building, completed in 1918, was based on a design by Shin'ichiro Okada. It sturdily maintained the flavor of academic classicism, whereas most of the other prewar Western-style structures built on Nakanoshima island, in the middle of Osaka, had one-by-one disappeared. As one of those who secretly hoped that the building might either be left intact or, better still, restored closely in accordance with the original design, I was skeptical of Ando's plan to plop a concrete egg into a staid and dignified assembly hall.

I could guess roughly what Ando was thinking. He would achieve a certain layering of past and present by directly inserting a pure geometric volume, such as this egg, into Okada's grand neo-Renaissance-style structure. The contrast, he must have believed, would bring out the best in both past and contemporary styles.

Engaging a contemporary architect to preserve or renovate a historic structure can be tricky. Should he rein in his creativity too much, his participation in the project becomes marginal, but to assert his own manner too forcefully could disrupt all continuity between past and present, provoking censure. Considering such difficulties, the egg concept was not only practical but allowed for coexistence—an inspired design based on dissonances.

Ando's plan, however, was not adopted. Several years passed, and I had mixed feelings: it was too bad, in one sense, but in another I was relieved that the matter had ended in a straightforward renovation of the Nakanoshima building.

Then, Ando's egg scheme re-emerged rather unexpectedly in Inamori Hall at Kagoshima University in Kyushu. Within this structure, donated to his alma mater by the Kyoto-based Kyocera Corporation's chairman Kazuo Inamori, Ando's egg was actually born.

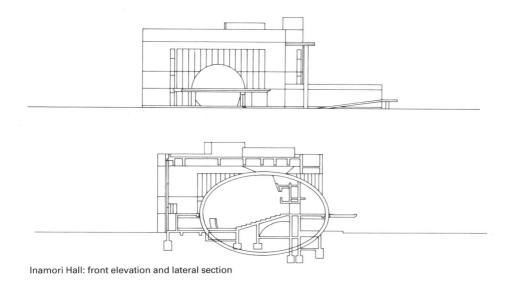

Inamori Hall: front elevation and lateral section

Inamori Hall is a lecture hall where visiting scholars and artists are invited to speak. The egg, nested squarely into the rectangular volume of the building, is the auditorium.

First, let us examine the structure's exterior.

Inamori Hall stands to the left of, and just inside, the main gate of Kagoshima University's Faculty of Engineering. Quite apart from the egg itself, it is a fine example of the beauty that contemporary architecture can achieve through a combination of concrete and glass. The extensive glass curtain wall of the main façade recalls the architecture of Mies van der Rohe in scale and boldness. From within the foyer, gazing at the trees outside, you begin to feel a new appreciation for the kind of space that modernists sought, for Ando has achieved a space ruled by simplicity, geometry, and clarity.

Then there is the egg-shaped capsule, which was built first as an independent structure from the rest. I am told that this procedure was adopted because of Inamori's insistence that the form be flawless. Were its geometry imperfect, the egg might have had to be reconstructed.

This work vividly expresses the will to embody rationality in the perfection of a geometric volume. It expresses both the client's and architect's conviction that a university is a seat of learning governed by intellect. In the end, the contractor, lavishing twice as much care and attention than upon any usual project, brought into being a perfect egg-shaped form that met the exacting standards of all.

Inamori Hall, Kagoshima University: entrance

Inamori Hall: auditorium interior

The inside of the egg is enfolding, like a womb. Yet this is the only place I know where one can experience the sensation of being within a perfect geometrical form, a body dictated completely by logic. And the optical fiber spots arranged concentrically about the inner surface of the egg create a dream-like regularity that further heightens one's awareness of the three-dimensionality of the space, intensifying its overall effect.

Sitting in the auditorium, you are filled with a sense of well-being. You feel keenly in tune with the universe, rather as if you were a particle suspended inside a model of a molecular structure. Inamori desired to arouse the minds of members of the university who come after him. Here people become conscious of being children of reason, exactly fulfilling the purpose for which the hall was endowed.

One is easily convinced that this "space of reason" has a life of its own. The egg shape, designed to confront history in the Nakanoshima Public Assembly Hall project in Osaka, has been realized in the southern prefecture of Kagoshima, devoid of historical context. Yet the determination with which Ando pursued the realization has served to enhance its achievement. His commitment motivated the builders, in turn, bringing into being a work I would place in the forefront of recent contemporary architecture. Considering all this, we can argue that here, too, history played a part in its birth.

# CITY

:::

The city is at one and the same time the architect's greatest challenge and the arena where his talents are best demonstrated. The issues he must address are many and varied, but certainly the architect's central task is to infuse the city with new energy and vitality, to heighten the level of its human and economic activities.

Urban architecture is expected to provide a lively and attractive setting and show to best advantage the prosperity of the metropolis. From such a perspective, the measure of a building's quality is how well it contributes to the greater vigor of the city and its inhabitants. Unfortunately, architecture does not universally produce this effect. In many instances a brand-new mammoth edifice rises up and snuffs out more intimate, smaller-scale sources of the city's energy.

Tadao Ando is a city boy. He was raised in Osaka, with the tumult of the town under his skin. He is perhaps less concerned with defending the honor of contemporary architecture than with trying to find out what the city needs. Recently, he has designed increasing numbers of public buildings, but until the mid-1980s the bulk of his work was urban and commercial in nature.

This is the architect who designed and built a public plaza against all conventional calculations of economic efficiency and who first made commercial nuclei of shops and boutiques into popular gathering places. No doubt it was a childhood spent playing in the streets that helped him redesign parts of the city to make them places where people would naturally congregate.

The city is a recreation spot par excellence and also a place to learn.

I believe only a person brought up in such a place is qualified to pass on the legacy of a truly liveable city, where successive generations can both play and learn. It is appropriate that such a place of recreation and learning possess a superlative spatial aesthetic. As an architect, Ando has acquired the practical skills to make this happen.

Ando's buildings do not attempt to flatter the urbanite; he concentrates instead on designing commercial structures where people will gather. At first drawing inspiration from the commercial developer Yasuhiro Hamano and ultimately developing fresh ideas of his own, he has produced a number of outstanding works in this genre. The commercial buildings Ando designs do greet the shopper or seeker of conviviality with a sterner look than is usual in this context, but even in the early days of his career, there was a stratum of user who sought the kind of high-quality, ascetic, unsentimental space that is Ando's.

Then, apparently having sensed the dangers lurking in the bubble economy's excesses, Ando began to move away from commercial architecture. In the last decade his only work in this genre has been Collezione (1989) in Tokyo. Sensing that the commercialization of urban space, which accelerated in the late 1980s out of all proportion to its economic value, was out of control, Ando withdrew from this genre that had once provided the bulk of his work.

Japanese cities were even then bursting with energy, but with the decline of department-store sales after the bubble collapsed, the tide of speculative money receded, and so did the footsteps of shoppers and the pace of consumption in the city. Architects anguished over how they might respond to this new trend, but the suspicion of developer schemes and rejection of urban lifestyle that spread through society at the time left them with few chances to redeem the name of the profession.

What can be expected of architects nowadays? Ando's response has been to tackle head-on the problem of how new architecture can reinvigorate and re-enliven the city. His Mermaid Plaza, built adjacent to the Suntory Museum in Osaka, was the first result. By negotiating with Osaka city hall, Ando succeeded in opening up a spacious area on the water's edge to public access and enjoyment by integrating his museum structure with the harbor-front at its feet.

Everyone was thrilled by this achievement. My own assumptions about the proper use of the city and public space had been shaped by Kobe's Motomachi district, as well as by the spacious foyer and restaurants of Junzo Sakakura's Ashiya Civic Center of 1963, so I had high expectations. But true success is rarely attained by creating work of such high artistic standards that it delights only the critics. Civic design is only complete if it encourages public gathering and interaction and if the spaces it creates enhance people's sense of identification with the city.

With the spreading impact of the virtual environment, we can foresee that the direct marketing of goods to consumers in stores or in shopfronts along city streets may be gradually eclipsed by online shopping. Commercial architecture is bound to change considerably by the turn of the century, and in the process of rethinking it, we need to rethink the city itself. How to sustain and invigorate the life of cities in the age of "virtual reality" is the issue we must now grapple with.

## Suntory Museum

As a loudspeaker blared out final departure, I raced down the pier—this time toward a tour boat—managing just in time to get aboard the already crowded vessel, fitted out like an old-fashioned sailboat. As it moved away from the wharf, I could see the entire waterfront: on the left Tempozan Marketplace and the Kaiyukan Aquarium, on the right the brand-new pastel-colored Hotel Seagull, and in the center Suntory Museum fronting Mermaid Plaza. Passengers lined the rails of the boat and gazed in wonder at the completely transformed image of the Tempozan waterfront.

The area had changed, a reality that lay before my eyes. Until a few years ago, this place was rarely visited except by those taking the commuter ferries across the bay; now it is one of Osaka's preeminent tourist attractions. This is popularly attributed to the presence of the mammoth new Kaiyukan Aquarium, but thanks are also due to Ando's museum and plaza complex. I sensed that each facility had now established its own identity and niche in the townscape and had begun to contribute to the city's vigor and prosperity.

Suntory Museum consists of a great cone, the IMAX Theater, and the art galleries. The former is a massive space for screening films in virtual three-dimension and the latter display the museum's permanent collection of poster art. From the bay, one sees the volume in which the IMAX Theater is nested, visible through the sloped glass walls of the building, and the cubical box beside it that houses the gallery facility.

The nested structure echoes Ando's proposal for Nakanoshima Pub-

Suntory Museum, Osaka, and Mermaid Plaza

Suntory Museum: the amphitheater looking seaward

lic Hall and his completed Inamori Hall in Kyushu. The gallery is a typical Ando-style plain box raised on stilts. As if holding hands, these two elements of the museum reach out to people who have come primarily to visit the Kaiyukan Aquarium, thus helping spin the engines of the district's new-found vitality.

It goes without saying that Ando poured heart and soul into conceiving this museum. But we should not overlook the fact that he devoted himself with equal energy to the Mermaid Plaza. This stretches along the waterfront at the foot of the museum, its contours firmly following the rules of Ando's aesthetic. The broad steps begin at the open area under the gallery wing of the museum and stretch all the way down to the water, sweeping outward to form a beautifully composed public space.

Sitting on these broad steps, you can see far, far out to sea in a westerly direction. This area, called Naniwa-zu in ancient times, recalls the introduction of Chinese civilization to our shores, near Japan's ancient capitals. More simply, it is across this stretch of water that one may enjoy the sight of what Ando believes to be the finest sunset in Japan.

Ando conceived Mermaid Plaza, as with a number of his recent works, in order to channel our vision outward toward a particular landscape. This is a creative aim he equates to the task of architecture itself.

In order to realize this space, Ando had to do battle with a many-tiered local and national bureaucracy whose areas of jurisdiction crisscross on the waterfront. The interests of a private firm like Suntory appear simple in contrast with the red tape one encounters in city and ministerial offices. Initially, use of the waterfront for any but long-established purposes faced innumerable obstacles. But Ando appealed persistently to city hall and other agencies for cooperation in creating this public square, finding in such work the true mission of an architect. Indeed, he maintains that today the architect must not only build isolated structures beautiful in themselves, but also coordinate other points of view, thereby realizing spaces that are truly public.

The challenge corresponds to the wider battle to ease or remove government restrictions throughout urban Japan. The idea that an individual architect can take the lead, setting an example, shows a remarkable degree of positive thinking, considering that public faith in the profession remains at an all-time low since the bubble. His sort of approach is much needed at a time of widespread public indifference to the needs of the city, owing in part to the communications revolution that seems to accelerate this disregard.

Our tour ship returned to the wharf at Tempozan after circling Osaka Bay. In the slanting rays of the setting sun I could see that there were now even more couples dotting the steps of Mermaid Plaza than earlier. To be sure, the hour was only moments away from one of Ando's superb sunsets.


## Step

Few of the younger generation in Japan are aware that one of our country's best showcases of contemporary architecture is the somewhat remote city of Takamatsu on the island of Shikoku. Along its streets are to be found a number of important works, including Kenzo Tange's Kagawa Prefectural Office, built during the days when modernism was at its most confident.

Ando's first imprint on this city was a modest commercial building completed in 1980 called "Step." With a frontage of some thirty-two feet, it is a mere "pencil" building that nevertheless contributed significantly to Ando's reputation early in his career. The theme of this work is echoed in its name: Step. A four-flight range of stairs rises through the center of the slender structure, dividing it in two. The vertical passageway is unroofed, open to wind and rain.

Evidently, the concept repeats the principle Ando pioneered in his light court in Sumiyoshi Row House. In that earlier work, the design is premised on the inhabitant as nature-lover stranded in the city, and the composition imposes the inconvenience of an umbrella in getting from one part of the house to another during inclement weather. Step inflicts similar inconvenience on shoppers browsing the building's boutiques and shops.

The exposed reinforced concrete of Step is simple of mien. Amid the gaudy advertising of its neighbors in this arcaded shopping street, the building is retiring and even a little difficult to find. Yet Step won high praise at a time in the 1980s when people were searching for something beyond mere material affluence, and it helped propel Ando into the architectural limelight.

The day I visited Step, it happened to be raining quite hard. It seemed dark as I climbed the steps under my umbrella, yet I noticed quite a few young women moving in and out of boutiques, umbrella in hand.

At the top of the stairs was the Ando universe, notably different

◄ Suntory Museum: looking outward with the shell of the IMAX Theater at left

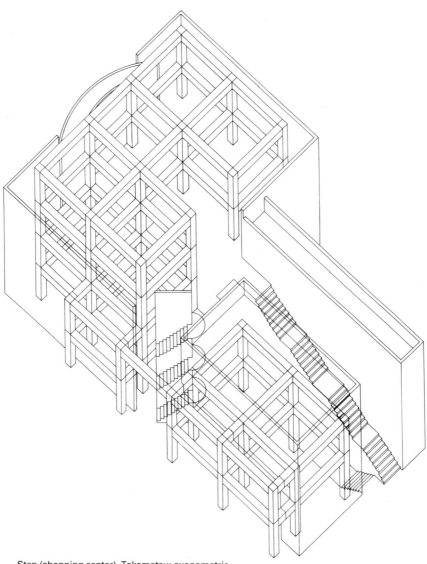

Step (shopping center), Takamatsu: axonometric

Step: pedestrian access from street level ▶

Step: night view from above

from the bustling arcade below. Its polished spaces of exposed concrete attracted smart women shoppers pursuing their heart's desires. Had they come, I wondered, on some stray mention of Tadao Ando, to shop at this "inconvenient building"?

In retrospect, Step displayed both the best and worst of Ando's youth at this time: an all-too-blatant concept and an undisguised modernist feeling. In a way, it was a reckless adventure. But the arbiters of architectural taste liked what they saw.

Japan had achieved prosperity, consisting above all in the balance of payments surplus, and was agonizing over a turn from the pursuit of material affluence toward a renewal of concern for the quality of life. It happened that the aggressive stance of Ando, a rising young star in the world of architecture, matched the tenor of the times. His impetuosity caught my critical eye. I saw Step as an ambitious attempt to apply the Sumiyoshi Row House experiment to commercial architecture and thereby enhance the quality of space.

I remember Ando swearing that people would climb that long flight of steps. And in fact, the number who did so was considerable, stirring the architect to challenge further the convention that people would only enter a shopping precinct if there were escalators or elevators. The media supported him, and articles explaining the concept were read by architects throughout Japan.

Step was a success for Ando in many ways. Of all the commercial facilities he built in his early career, no other presents his ideas so articulately. It brought him to the attention of the fashion industry, moreover, and paved the way for a spate of commissions from well-known manufacturers.

The work was also noticed by well-placed advocates of modern architecture, such as Kagawa prefecture governor Masanori Kaneko, who had been instrumental in bringing Tange and other modernists to Kagawa. He was delighted by Step, and it is said that he also paid several visits to Ando's subsequent work in Takamatsu—Sun Place (1982)—following the progress of its construction with satisfaction.

Today it is hard to say how much Step really contributed to Takamatsu's vitality. We may remember it, nevertheless, as a work that triggered a major shift in priorities. Buildings in this genre stopped flattering and fawning on shoppers, seeking instead to offer them quiet, tasteful spaces, perhaps even suggesting ideas about the nature of space and design.

The fact that such a modest building as Step helped set the tone for

Sun Place (shopping center), Takamatsu: detail of entrance

Sun Place: detail of skylight

Sun Place: detail of concrete

commercial architecture in the 1980s is rather amazing. In a sense, those were the "good old days," especially considering the present situation, when architecture has relinquished its vanguard stance in the aftermath of economic downturn.

## Rose Garden

Commercial architecture can breathe vitality into a city, but it can also plant the seeds of decay. In our time, commerce is the single most powerful force bringing people together in cities. The problem we face is how far commercialism should be allowed to hold sway. If taken too far, the city is reduced to little more than a fantasy theme park.

Ando's Rose Garden (1977) took a stand on this issue. It was this work, which I happened to see while visiting old houses in the Kitano district built by Western residents in Kobe's early years, that opened my

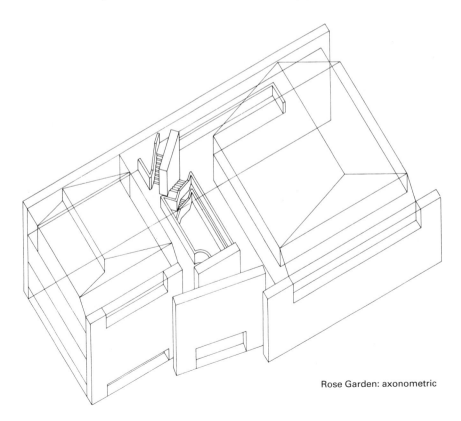

Rose Garden: axonometric

Rose Garden: exterior wall with projecting lintels

Rose Garden: detail of open circulation area

eyes to an appreciation of contemporary buildings. The sight is imprinted on my memory, for I discovered there an ideal of commercial architecture. The corridors and inner courtyard at Rose Garden appeared, to an eye inured to the excesses of commercialism, a refreshingly natural space.

It was in the days before the Kitano tourist boom, which was occasioned by a popular TV drama set in the area, and there was as yet almost no place to sit and rest. Trudging about these streets of venerable residences, I had begun to feel a little irritated not to find a public square or some other vantage point from which the wider pleasures of the town could be savored. When at last I arrived by accident in front of Rose Garden, I was delighted by the liveliness of its brick-tiled façade. Passing through the narrow entry, which reminded me of traditional buildings in Europe, I reached an inner courtyard and my irritation quickly dissipated. Each upper floor being ringed by a corridor, the natural concrete of balconies contrasted strikingly with the brick-tile walls, smartly delineating the entire space. This pleasant courtyard offered a repose such as I had never experienced in contemporary architecture.

The scene made quite a picture. On a chair pulled out into the middle of the space sat a silver-haired accordion player, apparently European, playing with verve against the backdrop of a florist's shop. I no longer remember the audience clearly, but some people had paused to look and listen from the galleries above. Yet, in memory, I carry the vivid impression that the accordionist was playing for me alone.

That scene held a charm quite different from the blatantly commercial American-inspired shopping malls I was familiar with. It exuded a sense of foreignness and serenity such as you only find in a place like Kitano, part of a city whose history goes back to the days of the so-called treaty ports, which were first opened to foreign trade in the mid-1800s. The experience initiated my critical study of Ando's work. I was favorably impressed by an architecture that seemed to me to contribute conscientiously to what the city was about.

Should commercial architecture get increasingly out of hand, we would inevitably be left with a late 1980s-style Las Vegas. Ando's Rose Garden, built back in the 1970s, admirably achieved a restraint still needed today. It brought elegance and character to the townscape and people responded in kind, which is what made possible the accordion player's performance.

Some years later, when the old Western-style buildings, some converted into restaurants or museums, had made the area a major tourist spot, Ando's Rose Garden became a natural model for the shops and other commercial establishments that flocked to cater to the new needs of the town. Ando has erected eight works in the neighborhood, and many more have been built by other architects in similar fashion. The precedent Ando set—a courtyard with tenant shops arranged around it— was copied and adapted over and over, offering a unifying theme for commercial sites in today's Kitano.

Here, too, Ando succeeded admirably in bringing the city vitality, contributing immeasurably to a reawakened interest in this old foreign residential quarter that for some time had gone neglected. These unassuming buildings, as we have seen, forged an inextricable bond between Ando and the city of Kobe. Even today, two decades after completion, Rose Garden's brick-tile façade remains attractive and well preserved, further proof of its sympathetic quality as a work of townscape.

## Rin's Gallery

My first visit to Rin's Gallery was on an autumn day long after sunset. It was sometime in the mid-1980s and the town was teeming with young women shoppers. Lit by spotlights, the building shone brightly.

I believe this is the final work in which Ando made use of brick tile. Its profile I found fascinating, shaped by corridors and a small, pleasantly open patio. The corridor at the top of the narrow stairs is reminiscent of a long, deep alley, hardly the kind of space often seen in commercial architecture. Rin's Gallery was built at about the time Ando was shifting his focus to public architecture, and it is the last of many outstanding commercial buildings of his early period. Nothing could have been more suitable, it seems to me, than the gabled roofline Ando designed to face the steep road in front of the site. This gentle but distinctive architectural flourish evokes the stylishness and good taste Kobeites have prided themselves on since the city was founded.

Later I visited Rin's Gallery in the daytime and sat in the terrace café and, mindless of the bright sun, watched people going up and down the slope outside. For a person like me, born and raised in a suburb with many hills, it was a restful and nostalgic setting. If carefully designed commercial buildings like this one were to be built elsewhere, small and compact, surely the quality of urban space in Japan would improve.

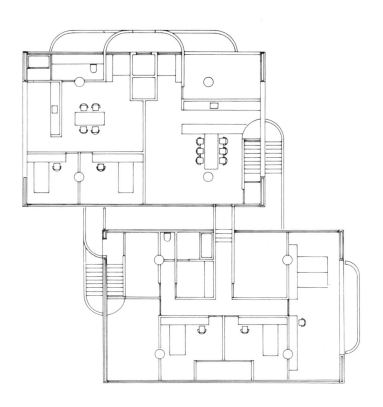

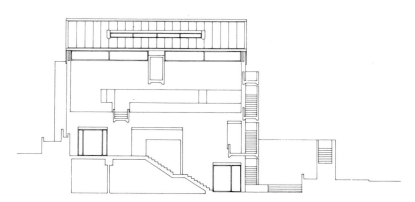

Rin's Gallery, Kobe: plan and lateral section

Rin's Gallery: gabled street façade and slope

Several months after the January 1995 Kobe earthquake, I returned to Kitano and saw Rin's Gallery again after more than ten years. The brick tile had acquired the patina of age, and the passage of time seemed to have made the exposed-concrete elements of the façade more attractive as well. Most contemporary buildings are at their best immediately after completion, degenerating from that point on, yet from all I could see, Rin's Gallery was aging well in the embrace of Kitano's distinctive townscape.

The quake did not damage this building, though reconstruction and repairs were underway in the surrounding town. As I walked up the steps after so many years, I noticed that the treads of the brick-tile steps were worn down by the footsteps of countless visitors, in the manner of a European cathedral porch.

In early 1996 I again visited Rin's Gallery, accompanying Ando as he consulted someone about expanding his Green Network movement in Kitano. He was here to gather support for his campaign to plant white-flowering trees, both as an encouragement to people rebuilding after the disaster and as a living memorial to the 6,000 persons who perished in the quake. Ando said he wanted to plant 500 specimens throughout Kitano. On account of the destruction of the Sannomiya

Rin's Gallery: circulation space

area, Kitano's closest access point by public transport, the stream of tourists and shoppers had slowed to a trickle, but shopkeepers and galleries had not given up and were attempting valiantly to reestablish business. Ando's call for backing was a further gesture of support. It was not about sentimentalism; it was designed to achieve a real purpose.

The image of the city immediately after the quake will remain in my memory forever. Sitting at the café with Ando as he attended to business, I gazed out at the city. People went about their affairs as if nothing had happened, but I was sure their hearts bore scars more terrible than anything a Tokyo-resident emigrant such as myself could imagine.

What had Ando's building seen on that tragic day? It was certainly witness to the blaze that left the very heart of Kobe burned out and to the pain and anguish of the many left homeless or injured. A building cannot tell its story but can only keep silent counsel as the years go by, festooned by white blossoms each spring.

Neither I, when I first visited Rin's Gallery, nor this building when newly built could have foretold the disaster that took place on January 17, 1995, but one can envision without difficulty how the scene will look as the years pass, surrounded with trees that symbolize sorrow for those lost and metaphorical rebirth for the living. It seemed to me there could be no better place for this appeal. With its unchangingly gentle architectural expression, Rin's Gallery has endured and survived the contingencies of Kobe's recent history and is a source of strength. I hoped the gallery would help the town sustain its vigor and that Ando would build there again.

## Collezione

Coming out of Omotesando Station and walking in the opposite direction from the young-people's trendy shopping mecca of Harajuku, you find one of Tokyo's most cosmopolitan and stylish fashion quarters, dotted with expensive boutiques and cafés. The street is lined with buildings housing Comme des Garçons, Y's and other designer brands, the respected patissier Yoku Moku, and the Tessenkai Noh theater, all quite attractive from an architectural point of view.

Ando's Collezione is a more recent addition, built on a corner at the far end of this district. Its gray exposed concrete and typical Ando air set it apart from other buildings, which seem instead to compete with one another in the conspicuous elegance of their designs.

Collezione is not overlarge, but once inside you feel the complexity of a city in the intertwining network of corridors and courtyards tucked into structural voids. The footprint of the building is determined by the intersection of two streets at a slightly greater than ninety-degree angle. Ando then inserted a prominent cylindrical core.

Within the cylinder and clustering around its circumference are various fashion boutiques, their interstices filled with steps and open courtyards. Indeed, the visitor can seldom see what lies ahead. Relying upon the sheer concrete to right and left, you pass obediently, somewhat dubiously, along the path Tadao Ando has determined.

Moreover, since the structure extends below grade, after you have wandered through corridors and up and down steps for a while, you may find you have quite lost all sense of where you are. On the building's south side is a courtyard space of double height, and only here do you begin to grasp the scale and logic of the building.

All this affords an intriguing experience from the perspective of spatial encounter. For example, as you ascend the steps arranged about the cylindrical concrete well, you suddenly discover brightly lit show windows at eye level on either side. After the confinement of the passage-

Kitano Alley, Kobe: gabled interior

Kitano Alley: rooflines

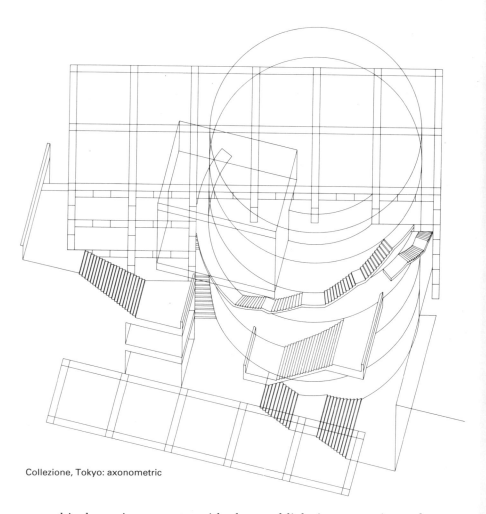

Collezione, Tokyo: axonometric

way, this dynamic encounter with glass and light is an experience that would be hard to match in any other building.

In general, the sensations here are of traversing the narrow lanes of a medieval town. Much of the pleasure of wandering through winding streets is being able to browse through shops and pause in cafés along the way. For European townscapes, such shops and establishments are indispensable accents, and the corridors of Collezione offer the Tokyo-ite a similar experience. As you pass through corridors and up and down steps leading you know not where, bright spaces along the way evoke the traditional city.

We must not forget, however, that Collezione is governed by a very twentieth-century notion of space that sets it apart from the ordinary urban hustle and bustle. There is a tremendous difference between the

Collezione: curved wall and recessed floor lighting ▶

tumult of a typical local marketplace and the aplomb of Collezione. There are no sidewalk stands typical of most Tokyo shopping streets to entice shoppers inside. Collezione, and each shop within, primly and discreetly awaits the arrival of customers. This sort of mini-emporium could be called snobbish, yet commercial buildings with this degree of refinement are hard to come upon in any city in the world.

Coming from Omotesando Station, you perhaps noticed, as you passed the Comme des Garçons boutique, that it was illuminated only with fluorescent tubes. In the same way, the interior of Ando's building is lit throughout with pale daylight lamps heightening the inorganic and rarefied image of Collezione. The combination of concrete labyrinth and gigantic plate-glass windows, so unlike real shopping streets, may be called the culmination of the twentieth-century city. I believe that the metropolitan qualities of Collezione are memorable in part because there are so few other examples of the genre.

The commercial work Ando produced in the 1970s-80s established his reputation as an architect of the city—almost as an urbanist. Collezione is an extension of those earlier endeavors, but it also clearly differs in scale and texture. What makes this building a landmark in Ando's career is its proof that the architect has refused to abandon his original commitment to the ideal of twentieth-century urban space.

◀ Collezione: atrium

Collezione: street façade

# EPILOGUE

## Return to Row House Sumiyoshi

⬛⬛⬛
⬛⬛⬛
⬛⬛⬛

The entire townscape has changed, but after all, nearly twenty years have passed. My first visit had been on a winter evening, and I vividly remember the brightly colored neon signs that lit up the darkness in the old entertainment district. I was still in my twenties, and Ando's star had only begun to rise in the architectural firmament. Unlike today, his name was not known by every man and woman in the street.

For that first trip, I believe, we came down to Sumiyoshi, which is in the southern part of Osaka, from Ando's office in the central Senba shopping district. At the time, I had yet to write my first article about modern architecture. I had visited his office because I was intrigued by the originality of Ando's ideas on city living.

I remember passing through the reddish neon-lit district and coming into a quite different, largely residential community composed of somber-hued, two-story wooden houses. Charcoal-black tiled roofs—gable ends facing the street—lined the alleys where the playing of children echoed until darkness fell. This was still the kind of traditional Japanese townscape you might expect to find in a woodblock print or an Ozu film.

Such was the townscape into which Row House Sumiyoshi was born in 1976, rising in stark concrete between a pair of wooden structures in the vernacular row-house style, as those of the Ando faithful will know. Hemmed in on both sides by the old-fashioned, endearing dwellings loved by ordinary Osakaites, Ando's concrete box remained a definite oddity.

You might call it dour or you might call it determined looking. However you describe it, what Ando introduced to the townscape was an anomaly, modernism face to face with indigenous Japan. And yet, from another viewpoint, one could conceive the relationship of concrete box and old-style row houses as a mutual rivalry to represent the spirit of Japanese-style architecture. Ando's building asserted that the essential spirit of Japan is *mu*, which depending on the context means "nothing" or "void." Yet, the surrounding buildings seemed to insist that they, as anyone could clearly see, were the real embodiment of the Japanese tradition.

To return, however, to our twenty-year reunion last winter with Row House Sumiyoshi. Ando and I arrive to find the neighborhood transformed. When I voice my astonishment, Ando's expression shows he feels the same.

"It certainly has changed. Nothing like before . . ."

Row House Sumiyoshi is located one street behind the main thoroughfare. The first thing we had noticed is that wooden structures were all but gone from along the main street. In their place are semi-prefab apartments built with lightweight pre-cast concrete panels. The concrete, moreover, is not the usual gray; the town has been painted disconcerting hues of maroon and pink. The quiet intimacy long sustained by the dark, weathered tones dominant in the old townscape has vanished.

Thinking about density and building-to-lot ratios, I ask Ando, "This area is 60/200, right?"

"Well, I thought that's what it was. I wonder if they get enough sunshine."

The block facing Row House Sumiyoshi had been completely rebuilt with three-story structures. Ando appears skeptical that a fair amount of sunlight could now reach the north side of the street. I am dismayed to see so many three-story intruders, and amazed at how completely they alter the townscape. Of the two houses flanking Ando's row house, that on the left has been rebuilt as a three-story, concrete-panel-wall structure, like so many other houses in the area. The old row house on the right is one of the few around that has not been rebuilt, though it now sports a gold-colored aluminum-sash bay window on its second floor.

"It was better all row-houses," Ando grumbles defensively.

My memory goes back to what the neighborhood was like before. Back then, when Ando's concrete box materialized, its roofline was just a bit higher than the other houses. Now it is lorded over by three-story dwellings.

Actually, I had been under the impression that Japan had not changed all that much over the past twenty years. Already back then we had the "bullet" super-express trains, not to mention jumbo jets. Even the recent deluxe Nozomi (Hope) super-super express has only sliced thirty minutes off cross-country travel in those two decades, and though new planes have given us more direct flights to Europe and the U.S. East Coast, the trip still seems long and uncomfortable. You wonder at times whether twentieth-century progress has more or less leveled off.

But in fact, events have moved apace. Two decades ago, our traditional Japanese lifestyle was on the way out. Uncluttered tatami-floored spaces, open to the out-of-doors, secluded back gardens, and cozy courtyard gardens were already a dying species. The townscape that lies before me now shows that the trend has unmistakably progressed further.

Observing the progress of reconstruction in the wake of the Hanshin earthquake, Ando fretted that Kobe was destined to become "the largest prefab city in the world." Frame buildings suffered the worst fate in the earthquake's forceful tremor, so it was easy to understand the overwhelming preference for concrete paneling and prefabs today. But even before the earthquake, it had been clear to Ando and myself in Sumiyoshi that the indigenous, distinctively Japanese lifestyle would soon disappear from these streets. Nor was there any way to turn back the tide.

Ando rings the bell at Row House Sumiyoshi and the hospitable Azumas welcome us inside. This home is truly beautiful, only the concrete walls having darkened a little over the years. Ando had originally split the limited floor space of the house (the site was only 645 square feet to begin with) by the "light court" on the ground floor and the connecting bridge. So the plan consists of four separate rooms, each a minimal space in itself. But the living room the Azumas show us into is so skillfully arranged that one is not the least conscious of its small size. Each piece of furniture fits its role, and the room is neat and attractive—almost spacious.

Although unlike most houses and some offices in Japan, this is a "shoes-on" household, it is so beautifully appointed that even Japanese guests need not take off their shoes to feel perfectly at ease. I have come thinking that I would ask some questions about the design of the house, but the conversation is so animated and lively that I begin to think that architectural issues no longer matter.

"How old is your dog now?" asks Ando, referring to the beagle padding slowly around the room, wagging its tail. "Thirteen." The dog goes up to the kerosene room-heater and sits. When I start to pat his head, he at once stretches out, resting his weight against my knee, and goes to sleep.

"You're a dog lover, right?" I comment to Ando, whose current dog, named "Le Corbusier," is a close companion at home as well as in the office.

"Oh, I like both cats and dogs," he answers.

I boast that my own black-and-white cat, Giovanni, was included in a photograph collection of "Cats Residing in Tokyo," published in 1995 by Treville.

We enjoy our visit immensely. Beyond the plate-glass wall, I can see into the courtyard, light filling every part of the space with a soft glow.

Over and over I have written of the "sternness and severity" of Ando's architecture. Out of attachment to a small plot of land and perhaps to the city itself, a few clients choose deliberately to build in relatively low-cost poured concrete, carving out the optimal dwelling within the space and means available. There are even some architects who elect this lifestyle, but it takes a special resolve and conviction for most people to commit to living their daily lives in a small, or large, dwelling of monolith concrete. I frequently visit Ando's residential works just prior to their occupation, and I often find myself worrying what it would be like to actually live in them.

Ando has told me of the various difficulties the Azumas have been through with this house, and he himself admits that in general making such a house livable is no easy task. In summer it becomes extremely hot, and in winter the rooms are extraordinarily cold. No doubt these twenty years have been much occupied with meeting and overcoming each challenge to livability posed by the architect's design.

I feel happy indeed for the Azumas, seeing the comfortable and elegant life they have built in this not-very-large dwelling, divided four ways. The utter relaxation of the dog leaning against my leg is proof. The total abandon you find only in animals that are loved and cared for is evident in the uninhibited weight of the beagle against my knee.

The term "severe" will not do for the Azuma house as it is today. Moreover, I would hesitate to claim that it was only Ando's light court that produces the feeling of genuine relaxation we experience there. On the contrary, it has a great deal to do with the dedication of the owners who have so admirably mastered the art of living comfortably in an austere modernist box. Each room is graced by not one item in excess, a style of living not easy to achieve, whether in Japan or the United States, in our materially over-endowed times. And what impresses me even more is that this lifestyle is completely natural, based on obvious choices of daily life, without any pretense at artistic statement.

Ando is to be envied. What a fortunate man and a lucky house-builder! In the two decades of my preoccupation with architecture I have seen much of the mismatch between architect and client and its harvest of rancor. There has not been a single other case in my experience without trouble.

But the Azumas have solved every problem at Row House Sumiyoshi. I do not know any other home where the beauty of a unique lifestyle communicates itself so eloquently, although hardly at a spoken level. The house itself is one that most today would recognize as among Ando's most important. But it is significant not just because of its modernist concept, the beauty of its ultra-simple exterior, and the idea of a light court. Rather, its total expression, complemented by the daily life of its owners, is art itself. To me this is inspiring and rare.

Few architects are fortunate enough to see their work age and endure so fruitfully over so many years. This blissful time is the Azumas' gift, and for those gathered an exquisite feeling of pleasure enlivens the conversation.

Mrs. Azuma says, "The local policeman comes around and says, 'Is this what they call the Row House Sumiyoshi?' And when we say yes, he remarks, 'You mean, it's only *this*!'"

"So, it's got quite a reputation!" chuckles Ando, and we all laugh.

The already dim winter sun soon dips behind the city's horizon, bringing dusk and telling us that the time has come to take leave. But before we go, I have one wish. "Please let me cross your bridge," I say.

As I open the full-length glass doors and go out into the light court, the rush of cool air is refreshing. I climb to the second floor by way of the stairs on one side. The light court, landmark of Ando's career and device for sensing and savoring nature within the city, is enfolded by concrete walls on both sides. It all exists as if two decades had not really passed. Standing on the bridge, I momentarily sense the essence of the real time this space has passed through.

Loathe to leave, I descend slowly, returning to the living room. I find Ando and the Azumas planning something. Ando and I had thought we would go to eat in Minami, the popular entertainment district in central Osaka, but the Azumas want to invite us out to dinner.

"You don't mind *okonomiyaki*, do you?" queries Ando.

"Of course not."

"Good. But can we get seats? It's always crowded, and this is Saturday," worries Mrs. Azuma.

"Then how about 'Gen-chan's'?" interjects Mr. Azuma. "We can make reservations there." And, to Ando, "How about Western food you can eat with chopsticks?"

So the four of us go to eat, walking some ten minutes through the prefab-filled streets to "Gen-chan's."

"What is a restaurant like this doing here?" asks Ando, as we arrive at the Western-style restaurant situated in a totally Japanese neighborhood.

"Well, after all," explains Mr. Azuma, "this was once the red-light district. Uptown visitors to the district used to eat here when out on a spree, I'm told. We have sushi shops, and a French restaurant, too."

"Ando's Izutsu House is located here too, isn't it," I say.

"Anyway, the old geisha houses have completely disappeared from Sumiyoshi," Mr. Azuma tells us.

And here was "Gen-chan's" in a spot you might never expect such an establishment. After our walk through the town, marveling at its transformation, the food tastes superb. I enjoy myself thoroughly, genuinely happy. It is a luxury to visit, with the architect, a couple who have lived continuously in a house built for them twenty years before, and then to receive their invitation to dinner, indulging ourselves further by giving into their hospitality.

Having said our farewells to the Azumas, Ando and I catch a taxi. We are feeling a bit sentimental.

"Aren't they a wonderful couple," I say. "It's been twenty years since you built that house, twenty-five since you started your office. How many buildings have you designed in that time?"

"The Azumas are really good people. At the office, you know, each project involves about thirty staff, that many for a single building. But it's fascinating. Yes, it's been twenty-five years—we've completed about 200."

"If you figure it in aggregate, that's a human factor of 6,000 people's labor."

"Yes, you might add it up that way. And the network of relationships spreads further with each project. That's what makes it interesting." And there are all sorts of people. We really enjoy that. That's what makes design work so satisfying."

"Now, though, times are hard on architecture and on architects."

"Yes. It's really hard," says Ando. "During the bubble architects used to appear on television a lot. It was quite the fashion—but nowadays, we never do. That's how it was, but actually it's now that architects ought to be taking a stronger line on the city. We should be speaking up more. That's why I have been so vocal about post-quake reconstruction in Kobe. The authorities may curse me, but I say what I have to say."

Ando has remained active in the debate on rebuilding after the Hanshin earthquake. Working with the Housing and Urban Development Corporation, he is designing a 2,000-household housing project at the eastern end of Kobe harbor. At its start this fourteen-story complex will allot 500 square feet per dwelling, but as quake survivors get back on their feet, the units will be upgraded by combining two units into a single 1,000-square-foot apartment.

"We've got to build new public parks and public bathhouses. Many victims of the quake are older persons living alone. They shouldn't stay holed up by themselves. The only remedy is to create places where people can socialize," Ando argues.

Our taxi cruises a sea of neon signs, heading back toward central Osaka. Gazing out, I feel reassured. The jungle of rooftop signs and laundry poles somehow affirm that the warm gregariousness of the people who make up this city is slumbering in the darkness.

Architects have the means to do a great deal for city people, though the job of a critic is sometimes frustrating, about as satisfying as attempting to scratch your toe through your shoe.

In an age of virtual reality, people lament that building the millennial city is "difficult." Ando decries all this as gutless. He lambasts the waste of speculative money during the bubble era and urges that action be taken to pick up the pieces intelligently. I only hope that the force of his commitment will be appreciated.

In another twenty years what will Japan be like? What will humanity be like? Perhaps Ando, too, is thinking along these lines, I muse, as we simultaneously fall silent.

# SOLO

In our times, architectural design is sometimes sheer drudgery. An architect must deal with an intricate web of rights and prerogatives, meet countless official regulations, and settle numerous other details before work even begins. All this can sap the vital energies of creativity, relegating architecture merely to what can be squeezed from repeated compromise. Moreover, buildings now seem fated to rapid and indiscriminate recycling, whereas they were once assured a lifespan of a century or perhaps a millennium.

Tadao Ando persists in his search for truth amid this daily struggle. Through repeated discussion and dialogue, he develops his ideas and shapes his forms until both architect and client are happy with the results, yet somehow also pursues the perfection of his own universe. And he does it all almost single-handed. Of course, he is loyally supported by an able staff, but he takes the lead, establishing the design, presenting the model, and approving changes, down to the smallest detail.

The boss who keeps an eye on such minutiae is now difficult to find. I have encountered countless businesses where the boss leaves everything to his staff, who perform rigidly and inflexibly to the vexation of everyone around them.

Tadao Ando Architect and Associates is today run in an orderly and well-managed fashion quite unlike its earlier days. This is an extraordinary contrast to the sloppiness and lack of discipline observable all around us in society. Ando's way of actively taking charge and personally involving himself in even the most mundane details has worked effectively to combat the tide of the times.

Since the end of World War II, Japanese society has sought through egalitarianism and faceless conformity to raise everyone to a middling status. The problem, however, is that this has created a mass of white-collar workers who are competent generalists but specialize in nothing. Now the spread of computers is challenging the very raison d'être of the white-collar work force, compelling us to reassess the nature of work. The area of undefined responsibility that was once the specialty of white-collar office staff decreases with each passing day. As a result, individuals must now assume responsibility from start to finish for every task related to their jobs.

The greatest truth we can learn from Tadao Ando is his basic view of society and human nature: you only become a mature individual when you devote yourself with enthusiasm to a task, no matter how small. As information technology overtakes every domain, setting information processing and electronic communication tools within the reach of all, we are at last able to see the importance of this elementary rule.

In our electronic age with its uprootedness and disembodied values, architecture is clearly struggling against the odds. However, my impression, from observing the mien of Ando's office staff, is that those who survive all the hardships will have equipped themselves to endure on their own.

Ando's career is now in its twenty-fifth year, and I have been fortunate to know him for some twenty of those years. Ando's design philosophy, which begins with stripping everything back to human scale, has never wavered. But over the last two decades, architecture and the city have undergone tremendous changes, and now—as architects ask how they can contribute to society—I am convinced that Ando's ideas and approaches suggest how we Japanese may re-establish true autonomy and integrity. It is my modest hope that these essays will provide an introduction to Ando's outlook for readers abroad.

The pilgrimage to great edifices has for centuries been a required rite of passage for any devotee of architecture. Visiting Ando's work over a number of years has been one of the most fulfilling experiences of my career. I have tried to record some of these journeys in the first part of this volume. By contrast, the second part offers my perspectives on Ando's architecture as I view it today. The essays were originally published in various magazines—*Kikan Approach* , *Diamond BOX*, *Taiyo* (The Sun), *Kenchiku Bunka* (Architectural Culture), *Shinkenchiku* (Japan

Architect), and *Trend Setter*. They have been substantially revised and reorganized for this volume. I remain grateful to the editors of these periodicals for the opportunity to appear in their pages.

I must also express special thanks to Mr. Tetsuo Kuramochi of Kodansha International for his careful attention to the production of this book, and above all to Mr. Tadao Ando, who has been a constant stimulus and source of inspiration to me through his architecture.

Modern Art Museum of Fort Worth, Texas: competition model with Kimbell Museum at rear; scheduled completion 2001

A NOTE ON THE PHOTOGRAPHS

In addition to the photographs by Tomio Ohashi, this book also contains photographs by the author, Kazukiyo Matsuba, and Tadao Ando Architect & Associates. Those by the author appear on pages 20, 22, 24, 41, 42, 110, 112, 143, 160, 162, and 180; those by the Tadao Ando office appear on pages 155, 165, 166, 203, and 204.